From Cradle to War:

'My First Three Decades, 1915-1945'

Dick in his high chair.

From Cradle to War:

'My First Three Decades, 1915-1945'

by

Dick Maurice

The Pentland Press Limited
Edinburgh · Cambridge · Durham · USA

© Dick Maurice 1998

First published in 1998 by
The Pentland Press Ltd.
1 Hutton Close
South Church
Bishop Auckland
Durham

British Library Cataloguing in Publication Data.
A catalogue record for this book is available
from the British Library.

ISBN 1 85821 563 3

Typeset by George Wishart & Associates, Whitley Bay.
Printed and bound by Bookcraft Ltd, Bath.

To my wife Anne
for giving me fifty years of
such a happy marriage

Contents

List of Maps

Foreword

Given my limit on words, in writing about Dick Maurice and his enthralling book, I could choose to be briefly polemical or personal. I plump for the latter, not merely out of preference but because the Maurices have always been the least pompous of families. They have a long tradition of serving the community, both in peace and in war. With their background and resources, they could have elected to become rich by investing and marrying well, pursuing lives of desperate triviality. Instead, they have devoted themselves to serving town, county and country – and nowhere more obviously than in medicine: the Marlborough practice must be one of the oldest, if not the oldest, in Britain.

I first encountered them in 1939 as one of five grubby evacuees from London. The kindness and tolerance of Dick's father and mother were beyond anything we had a right to expect (or I could provide myself in similar circumstances). Though we all came from comfortable middle-class homes, in Marlborough we encountered something new: a quiet and stable community with a sense of purpose and continuity rather different from our jittery London suburbs.

Nevertheless, things have never stood still. Symbolically, today, where I remember a woodshed and sawmill providing logs for the great house there is a spankingly elegant and efficient health centre. And, needless to say, Maurices are still in practice there. Dick's memoirs reflect why this is so, and why it will almost certainly be so in another 100 years' time.

Stephen Lock

Preface

Most of us know little about the early years of our parents, let alone our grandparents. Here I have tried to remedy this for my descendants. Inevitably it is the war years that take up the greater part of what I write. For me the War, if it had to come, could not have started at a better time. As a senior medical student my call-up into the forces had to be postponed until after my qualification and then a year as a resident in a hospital. The Blitz on London in the autumn of 1940 was an unforgettable experience. It meant too that the normal barriers between consultants, hospital registrars, residents and students were broken down and we all pulled together in a way that would be unthinkable in peacetime. How different then was life in London – the entire population seemed welded together and out to help each other. It is interesting too how the friendships formed between us students have lasted all our lives; inevitably we got to know each other so much better than we would have done in times of peace.

Life in the Army is another experience which I would not have missed for anything. Doctors could at least continue to practice their chosen profession; our job was to heal – not to kill. Again I believe I was singularly fortunate – I am sure for me India and Burma provided much more interest than North Africa, Italy or the invasion of France could ever have done; and as I had no wife or children to worry about the long separation from home was of rather less consequence than it was for some. The camaraderie and friendships formed by the shared difficulties and separation meant so much to us all – and how fortunate I was in my four postings.

I have quoted at length from my letters home because I believe they do reveal that life in wartime, especially if lived through one's third decade, can be enjoyable. When I started to write these memoirs I did not realize how much I would enjoy reliving that decade of my life.

This book was originally typed and photostated for my descendants and for many of my old friends. I had no thought of publication until I read in the Burma Star Association journal that the Pentland Press specialised in this sort of work, so I got in touch with them and sent them a copy of my book. It was actually written in 1989.

Acknowledgements

First to my wife, Anne, who not only put up with me while I was editing the book but also suggested the main title should be *From Cradle to War*.

I am most grateful to Dr Stephen Lock for writing the Foreword. As a City of London School pupil he spent the war years as an evacuee at Lloran House while they played Cox and Box with Marlborough College. Perhaps it was the large house and garden which my family owned that made him think a medical career would be a rewarding one; and all those unopened *British Medical Journals* that littered the long table in the hall at Lloran House that led to his becoming for many years Editor of the B.M.J.

My thanks are due to my brother, Tim, who like my parents kept all the letters I wrote to him during the War.These are now all in the archives of the Imperial War Museum.

My thanks also to the Pentland Press for their encouragement when I sent them the original manuscript which I had typed in1989 and particularly to Mrs Mary Denton, the Publishing Manager, who has had to put up with all my telephone calls and requests for advice.

Chapter I

Early Years 1915-29

I was born on 15 December 1915 in a house situated only one half mile from the house in which I now live, in the old market town of Marlborough. The town has experienced a greatly increased population since the last war; it is now to some extent a commuter town for Swindon and even further afield, but it still manages to retain its character helped by the famous wide High Street which contains the bulk of the shops. It was in a house on this street that I entered the world, a house which my family had occupied for over one hundred years. Now as then the High Street is a great place for greeting familiar faces and old friends; I can still walk down it and meet those who would have attended my seventh birthday party sixty-seven years ago. I am not alone in putting down roots.

My family originally came from North Wales and can trace their origins there back to the thirteenth century. The Welsh did not adopt surnames until the seventeenth century and it was only then that Morus ap (son of) Maredudd had a son – David Maurice – that our surname became established. David inherited the family property of Lloran Ucha in Denbyshire as it was then called, near Llansillin. David's son Edward was

1

High Sheriff of Denbyshire in 1676 and it was David's great-great-great-grandson, Thelwall Maurice, who entered the medical profession, trained at St Thomas's Hospital and became partner to Dr Pinckney at Marlborough in 1792. It is his direct descendants who are still in the family practice to this day. My father was the fourth generation to enter the practice. He had spent eight years in the Navy as a surgeon and then joined his elder brother – Oliver – in 1910. There were eight other brothers. Sadly Oliver died in 1912 shortly after the death of their father and it was thus that my parents, who had married in 1911, moved into the family house named Lloran House after the ancestral home in North Wales.

My only brother, Tim, was almost four years older than me and so by the time I was three he was rising seven and we tended to lead separate lives. Mine centred round my nurse, 'Taylor' as she was called even by me; her Christian name was Mercia. She had been housekeeper to my mother's uncle, Henry Richardson, a retired housemaster at Marlborough College. Henry Richardson was always known to Marlburians as 'Old Dick'; my second name is Richardson and I have always been called Dick after him. Taylor must have been about sixty when she came to nurse me; I had an idea she was alive in the Crimean War. My mother was over thirty-six when I was born and in those days children only appeared in the drawing room after tea and otherwise were reared by their nannies; inevitably I was more bonded to Taylor than to my Mummy. I do not doubt that she spoilt me no end but our mutual devotion was enormous. My nursery looked onto the High Street and in my early days Taylor slept there with me, supplying my every want.

There were three other servants living in the house: a cook, a parlourmaid and a housemaid. Outside there were two full-time employees: Gunning, the chauffeur, general handyman, additional gardener and even butler on occasion, and Newman, the gardener. They lived in cottages bordering the upper end of the extensive garden which ran down to the river Kennet and beyond, we had a foot bridge over the river. On the far side of the Kennet there were allotments stretching up to the Pewsey road bridge and some of our vegetables were grown there too.

Yes, my childhood was a happy one. Taylor was always there to keep me occupied and I had plenty of toys although they were simple by today's standards. The view of the street from my nursery was a constant source of interest: the Town Crier with his bell, the gas man lighting the street lamps in the evening – no electricity in Marlborough in those days – and the cars and lorries passing through. I can just remember the army lorries in the High Street toward the end of the War and hanging out the flags on armistice night on 11 November 1918 and again the following year on peace night.

Inevitably my childhood friends were drawn from a limited circle. Marlborough was much smaller and class distinction much stronger in the twenties than today. William Golding lived on the Green and was the same age as my brother, but he was a pupil at the Grammar School where his father was a teacher and we did not know him. One good friend was Lawrence Bussell; his father had been chaplain at Marlborough College but had joined the Army in the War and had been killed. Peter Taylor was a great friend; he was exactly my age and his father joined mine in the practice shortly after the War. He and I played endlessly together; the seed box we still have in our garden shed was once part of a home-made lorry and has 'Dick Peter – London Ltd' crudely painted on it. London Ltd was to show how important we were. Then there were the O'Regans – John who was a little older than me, Michael who was a little younger and Patrick. Their father was a well-liked Marlborough College master who sadly died from a heart attack while on his way to Chapel on Prize Day in 1922. I remember John and Michael were sent to play in our garden that day; Patrick was too young and remained with his mother. Michael Hartigan was another friend; he was an only child and the son of the Hartigans who owned the racing stables at Ogbourne Maisey. I often used to be driven out by car to play with him; they had a young jockey who sometimes joined us for tea with Michael's parents. He lived in a bungalow on the Downs and we used to play in his garden too. There was always something rather special about Gordon Richards. My first schooling took place in the scout hut; this can have been little more than play school. My only memory is of a large sand tray on which we could build castles. After a spell in the Congregational

4

Church Hall we moved to the home of our teachers, Mr and Mrs Johnson Miller, in the London Road. They were a kindly couple who taught us to read and write.

Lloran House garden was a superb place in which to play; I still carry in my mind vivid pictures of it from end to end. My mother was a keen flower gardener and it was here she spent all her spare time. In addition to the flower borders there were plenty of vegetables and fruit in the main part of the garden running down to the Kennet. However I do remember Mr Newman, the gardener, complaining that 'Mrs Maurice keeps creeping on and creeping on.' It was here that I first had a pedal car and then a tricycle. I suppose I was about seven when I was given my first bicycle. It was very old, probably pre-war and painted black all over. In time I learned to ride it and well do I remember demonstrating my skill in front of Tim and a friend of his on the top lawn at Lloran House. I scrambled off after circling round once or twice and the thirteen-year-old with my brother took hold of the bicycle and gave it a great push. It travelled perfectly across the lawn into the side of the house where, horror of horrors, the front wheel buckled completely. Thereafter whenever I visited Slimbridge, I always hoped I should see Sir Peter Scott and be able to tackle him with the enormity of his offence that day. To give him his due I think he was contrite and would have remembered the incident.

In 1924 I was sent to boarding school – the Old Malthouse at Langton Matravers, near Swanage on the Isle of Purbeck. My brother Tim had already been a pupil there for four years, as was my cousin Alec who lived at Manton Grange. Peter Taylor, my great friend, started with me the same term; he was followed two years later by his younger brother, Freddy. I do not remember being unduly concerned at this severing of home ties, not even when it was time to leave and Tim could not be found; he was so unhappy at going back he had gone into hiding. Boarding preparatory schools were very different in those days but I think there was something rather special about the Old Malthouse; certainly I was happy there. Rex Corbett, the headmaster, was a kind though reasonably strict man and his wife, the daughter of a one-time bursar of Marlborough College, was a dear. The school adjoined another and rather larger preparatory school, Durnford, and Tom Pellatt, the headmaster, was a great character. His wife was the elder sister of Mrs Corbett. Tom Pellatt was something of a snob and he did his best to collect the sons of the good and the great although we had our fair share too. Durnford had some ninety boys, we about fifty. Both schools prepared their pupils for the major public schools: Eton, Winchester, Harrow, Rugby, Marlborough and in our case particularly, Dartmouth; in those days boys could opt for a naval career at thirteen. The school was in some respects very primitive: no electricity, just oil lamps. The loos were just earth closets in a hut with a tin roof; we sat on wooden thrones with no partitions between them and at the end pulled a lever on the back which deposited ash into the bucket. The dormitories were pretty sparse – the beds with their red blankets on top lined round the walls and basins with jugs of water on a bench down the middle.

The Old Malthouse still flourishes today and looks much the same from the outside; Durnford has long since ceased to exist. I have said I was happy there and so I was. Somehow the Corbetts, who had two boys of their own, the younger at Marlborough College, managed to instil a family atmosphere into the school. We were all known by and used among ourselves Christian names; this must have been almost unique in those days; I was never Maurice minimus! Mrs Corbett was a great help, she used to read to us in her drawing room in the evenings and where I learned my taste for Henty, Buchan and many other authors, indeed for reading in general. There were three other masters in the school: Mr Hinds, who was a bit fierce, Mr Woodhouse (Woody), who was a dear and Oliver Wyatt (Wyo), who was younger than the others and had served in the War. He had a car which we were able to travel in sometimes and went on to being a prep school headmaster himself after I had left the school. Then too there was Miss Adams, the matron and known to everyone as Sadie, a kindly soul to help mother us.

There were some aspects of school life I did not like – one particularly was the weekly dose of senna pods we were made to take each Wednesday night. After two years of this I complained to my parents – the only result was that syrup of figs was substituted with even more disastrous results every Thursday morning. In the summer we had a long mid-morning break when we ran down to the sea to bathe at the Dancing Ledge. This is a flat area of rock in which a pool had been blasted out by Tom Pellatt; the sea pours over the ledge at high tide and so the water in the pool is always fresh. But how I hated the run down to the pool on Thursday mornings when I frequently had to retire behind one of the numerous stone walls we passed on the way to relieve myself from the affect of the syrup of figs.

In those days opportunities to learn to swim were few and far between and at the age of nine I had never learned. New boys were taught to swim by being supported on a canvas belt on the end of a pole which was held over the water by one of the masters. This belt supporting our middles allowed free movement of the arms and legs, in some ways an improvement on the arm bands of today. Wednesdays and Saturdays were half holidays and in the summer we were frequently escorted down to the sea at Seacombe, the Dancing Ledge being reserved for Durnford, where those who could swim bathed off the rocks and we were given a picnic tea. Today the Dancing Ledge and Seacombe can be quite crowded with trippers; I never remember seeing anyone other than ourselves in those distant days. We never wore any sort of swimsuit and indeed possessed none. At Marlborough too we always bathed naked in the College pool and I have never really adapted to the wearing of swimming trunks.

We played the usual team games at the Old Malthouse – soccer in the autumn term and cricket in the summer; I never shone at either and was never a very enthusiastic player. In the Easter term we were able regularly to visit a wood in a valley below the school where we constructed huts out of wattle which was in plentiful supply. Also the soil was clay and we could put a lump onto the end of a stick and then switch it at an opponent; this was known as mud switching. On occasion we could take on Durnford.

Our health was cared for by Sadie and the local GP – Dr Baiss. Swanage had a cottage hospital but we were always just looked after in the school sick room. Although our numbers were so small two boys, George Churchill and Nicky Parker died in the sick room during my time in the school. No antibiotics in those days – I suspect they had pneumonia. I well remember the whole school being assembled on each occasion to be told of their death by the headmaster. Both George and Nicky had an older brother in the school at the time. Fortunately my own health was good, I had lost my appendix at the age of seven and apart from measles and occasional tonsillitis I had no real illness.

There were no half-term leaves at home in those days and I was only visited once each year by my parents when they would stay in Swanage for the half-term in the summer. We used to have a piece of paper on which we could count the days off until we could get home for the holidays. In 1926 we had a bonus: it was the year of the general strike and our Easter holiday was extended. My nursery at Lloran House was now my play room where I could indulge my passion for model railways. I had clockwork Hornby trains with stations, signals etc. In good weather there was always the garden to play in and the river where we had a punt and later a canoe. The water was navigable from the town mill to above the College and I spent many happy hours on it with my friends. We always had a dog too that required exercise and I used to enjoy my walks with him along Treacle Bolly to Preshute or up to Savernake Forest. Today I still do the same walks with a feeling of nostalgia, although Marlborough has grown so much it still has the lovely views from the forest and Granham Hill which do not look all that different. Often too I would accompany my father on his rounds. Few people owned cars and home visits were made much more frequently. Also there were far fewer doctors in outlying villages and patients were scattered over a much wider area than they are today. Frequent visits were made to Littlecote, home of the Wills family, to houses in the Pewsey Vale, to Tottenham House in Savernake Forest – home of Lord Ailesbury – to Ogbourne, Aldbourne, Chiseldon and all the surrounding countryside. I used to enjoy going with my father on these rounds and never minded sitting outside the houses in the open car; there was a hood which was put up when it rained. I remember my amusement once at Littlecote when a footman came out of the front door and directed a megaphone at the garages, originally stables, and shouted, 'Send round the best Rolls at once.'

Sometimes Tim and I would be taken away on a holiday by our parents, usually during April. I have a vivid memory of going to Buttermere in Wales. Alec and his father, my uncle Charles, came too on that occasion and we had wonderful walks over the mountains. Exmoor was another favoured place. Sometimes in the summer we might be taken to Cornwall and stay at Flushing on the other side of the Falmouth estuary with the Gards. Captain Gard was a retired naval surgeon and an old friend of my father. He had a boat and it was a great experience to go out mackerel fishing.

My aunt Nell lived with a Mrs Street who had been widowed in the War and had a son Jimmy who was about my age. They would sometimes take me on holidays to the West Country where we would stay in a hotel and I could be a companion for Jimmy. They had originally lived in Marlborough but then moved to Ewhurst in Surrey and I was sometimes made to go and stay with them there, rather against my will. However it was exciting when they took me to France and we had two weeks in a hotel near Dieppe, my first visit abroad.

CHAPTER II

Marlborough College and Cambridge, 1929-37

In 1929 I went to Marlborough College. Tim was in his last year as a home boarder as he was considered too delicate to board in the school following a very severe attack of measles shortly after he had started there. I went to A House, a junior house with Geoffrey Chilton as my housemaster. He was a bachelor as were all in-College housemasters at that time and had seen service in the War. He was a kind man and I remained happy there particularly as I could always get home easily. It was not parental ties but the fact that home was a marvellous place in which I could entertain my friends and escape from the inevitable community life of the College that made my initiation into such a large school so much easier than it must have been for some. It also resulted in my friends calling each other by our Christian names; I was horrified on arrival at the College to find surnames in use throughout the school. My mother was a good hostess both to my friends and to the many visitors that came to stay at Lloran House, some of whom were old friends who had sons in the school. Ned and Joan Williamson were among these; they had three sons and Ken, youngest of the three, was at Marlborough, although a little older than me and not in the same house. He is one among many who will figure later in these pages. As I went up the school I might entertain my friends to dinner in the evening and wine would be provided, not all that common in those days; Terence Milne was a particular friend and he reminded me many years later how another friend, Bill Parkinson, was heard to say, 'The one thing I like about the Maurices is that they have good food and plenty to drink.'

I do not intend to write at length about my time at Marlborough. I was not a great achiever and somewhat lacking in team spirit; I preferred the 'sweats' as we called them, runs over the downs, to rugby or cricket. After A House I moved on to B3 which had a young housemaster – E.G.H. Kempson. He was a keen mountain climber and also ran the College scout troop. The OTC (Officers' Training Corps) was compulsory but we were allowed to opt out in our last few terms if we wished and join the scouts. Here I must digress. My uncle Oliver who had died in 1912 had started scouting in Marlborough and district and my father took this over on his death. The local schools had no outdoor activities in the twenties and thirties and scouting was a wonderful way of introducing the young to the countryside. My father was made County Commissioner with overall responsibility for scouting throughout the county. At the end of May 1930 a scout rally for Wiltshire scouts was held on the playing fields of Marlborough College. Sir Robert Baden-Powell, as he then was, Chief Scout and founder of the movement, was guest of honour. I should have been back at school but was in quarantine for mumps and was able to attend the lunch my parents gave for him and be driven up to the playing fields in the procession of cars to attend the rally. Unhappily it poured with rain. B-P had been provided with a special oak armchair from Lloran House on which he sat to watch the event. He always wore a cloak over his uniform. All scouts wore shorts at that time, and I remember well the horror my parents experienced when they saw the polish on the chair had come off as a large brown stain on the back of the great man's cloak. After the rally I had an even greater thrill. B-P had a Rolls Royce which was affectionately known as the Jam Roll because it had been given to him by scouts from all over the world at an international jamboree. I was allowed to accompany Lady B-P and my father in this car to visit Mr Russell, the Marlborough scoutmaster, who was a patient in Savernake Hospital.

I was to meet Lord Baden-Powell as he became on a number of occasions after this with my father but he was not the only Boer War high-ranking officer I remember. Field Marshal Lord Methuen was also active in promoting the scout movement; he was a governor of Marlborough College and always lunched with us on Prize Day which included a governors' meeting. For some reason he insisted on being given rice pudding which I hated; I just had the fresh fruit salad. Field Marshal Lord Plumer had also been recruited into the scout movement by B-P. It so happened that in 1930 he was President of the MCC and in those days the

Marlborough-Rugby cricket match was played at Lords. My parents and I, and presumably also Tim, were invited to attend and to take tea in the President's box in the pavilion. I remember that tea well: we sat at small tables and at mine were Lord Plumer's sister and Ruth Turner, sister of the Master of Marlborough College. The Master himself was at a neighbouring table. During tea Lord Plumer's sister turned to me and asked, 'Who is the Master of Marlborough?' I was very embarrassed that she did not know when the Master's sister was sitting with us but kindly Miss Turner spoke up and said, 'My brother.' So far as I can remember this was the only occasion on which I have ever attended a cricket match at Lords – but then I have never again been invited to the President's box. It was toward the end of my time in my senior house that after my years in the Corps I was first able to become a scout myself. I much preferred the sort of activities they pursued to organized games, particularly the annual camps alternating between a site near Bridestowe on Dartmoor and at Capel-y-fin in the Black Mountains in South Wales. During my time at Marlborough I had developed another great interest – printing. A friend of mine who had come to live in the town and also attended Marlborough College was Tony Elverson; our mothers had been friends before they were married. Tony had acquired a little Adana printing press and he asked me to help him with it soon after I started at Marlborough. He lived at 10 The Green; it was a large house and we were able to establish our office on the third floor. Soon we found

15

this was a marvellous way of earning money; we could carry out small printing jobs for our relatives and the parents of our friends in the town. Postcard headings with the name, address and telephone number of the sender proved very lucrative and easy to print and we could invest our earnings in buying more equipment. I well remember my snobbish pleasure when we were asked to print 100 postcards for Lady Maclean, Tony's aunt. We had a titled lady on our books! I was not then to know that her son was to become the notorious Donald Maclean; even then he must have been at Cambridge and recruited into the Communist Party. We called our press the Green Tree Press and we also produced occasional issues of a small magazine which we called the *Marlborough Bird*. Mr Perkins, proprietor of the *Marlborough Times*, published an account of our activities which he concluded by writing: 'We shall have to look to our laurels.' So keen did I become on printing that I even thought of taking it up as a career instead of medicine, which I had always assumed would be my vocation. Group Captain Jones lived in the town; he had been commanding officer of and remained friendly with T.E. Lawrence – Lawrence of Arabia – during his time as Aircraftman Shaw. He showed Lawrence some of our work and as a result I had an invitation to visit Heinemann's printing works. I was given a conducted tour which finished in the basement where someone was doing a very humble job setting up type by hand. When I was told that he was a young Macmillan I decided I had better stick to the family trade of medicine.

It was in the Lent term of 1934, my penultimate term at Marlborough, that a young master asked me if I would help him to start printing as an activity in the school. Brian Hone was an Australian, a Rhodes Scholar who had obtained a cricket blue in his first year at Oxford, had captained Oxford in his third year and also taken up tennis and gained a tennis blue. He was a remarkable man because he was anxious to introduce activities for boys who had no interest in games. He had learned something about printing in Adelaide and at Oxford. In the Christmas holiday of 1933-34 he did a course of printing at the Shakespeare Head Press in St Aldgates and he obtained an old Albion hand press from the Oxford University Press. George Turner – the Master – gave him £100 out of his own pocket to purchase type and other accessories and so in the Easter holidays of 1934 we set up the College Press in an old condemned army hut on the parade ground behind the Memorial Hall. I brought type and machines from the Elverson home and Brian and I got to work. He was keen on fine printing on handmade paper and thereafter we printed quite often together during my vacations from Cambridge. The history of the College Press is well written up in a book edited by Richard Russell, head of the Oxford University Press, and published by the Whittington Press. The Hones, Brian and his wife Enid, became life-long friends. Brian returned to Australia during the War and became successively headmaster of Cranbrook School in Sydney and Melbourne Grammar School, and was knighted for his services to education in

Australia. He died in Paris while undertaking a European trip; he was to have spent a weekend with us and a party had been laid on when I read of his death in *The Times*. Sadly I missed the celebrations for the fiftieth anniversary of the foundation of the Press in 1984. I was asked to open an exhibition of work done by the Press but on that very day we were flying from Christchurch to Melbourne to stay with Brian's widow, Enid.

From Marlborough I went to Cambridge in the autumn of 1934 having been given a place at Pembroke College where Tim had preceeded me and which had a strong Marlborough connection. I remain very fond of Cambridge but am not sure I wildly enjoyed my time there. The pre-clinical subjects, anatomy and physiology bored me and I do not think that they were all that well taught by the very high-powered academics of the time. I did not work as hard as I should have done and had a guilt feeling that I should have been working harder. I had a bicycle, as no doubt all Cambridge undergraduates still do, and even in those days it was possible to get stopped in a traffic block. This happened to me one day when I was approaching Christ's College. Before the last war all cars had running boards to step on when getting in. There was a car beside me so I casually placed my foot on the running board to support myself on my bicycle. Suddenly I experienced a peculiar sensation in my head, almost as if my hair was going to stand on end. I cautiously turned my head toward the car beside me to receive a frigid stair from Queen Mary who was sitting in the back. My foot was hastily removed, I nearly fell over.

I did continue with my interest in scouting during my time at Cambridge and assisted in the running of a scout troop together with a friend of mine from Marlborough days who had also been a printer, Cyril Hooper. My two closest friends at Cambridge were Tommy Thomas and James Streatfeild. Tommy – Albert William Jesse were his baptismal names but even his parents called him Tommy – was a classical exhibitioner at Pembroke and was being tutored by a young don from another College whom he greatly admired. He was always talking about him but I thought he had a very strange name – 'Enoch Powell'. One summer vacation Tommy, James and I went on a trip to Germany. We went to Munich by rail, third class which meant sitting on wooden seats, and explored the mountains south of the city. In Munich we saw something of Hitler's brownshirts and did not like what we saw. On our last night in Munich we had virtually run out of money; I do not remember how it happened but the only bed I could get was a dentist's chair. Tommy joined the Colonial Service and was sent out to Malaya. When the Japanese invaded he insisted on leaving his office in Singapore and joining up; he was killed immediately. James Streatfeild also went into the Army and is reported as having died on active service in Malaya in May 1942, presumably as a prisoner of war. Sadly quite a number of my Marlborough friends were also lost during the War.

CHAPTER III

St Mary's Hospital and the Start of the War, 1937-42

In the autumn of 1937 I started work at St Mary's; I was to find clinical work much more exciting and rewarding than preclinical studies and soon I was enjoying myself enormously. Mary's had been built at the same time as the Great Western Railway had been constructed and it is close to Paddington Station. It was reasonably convenient to get to from Marlborough and I believe I was the ninth Maurice to enter St Mary's. Dr Charles Wilson, later to be Churchill's doctor and to be made Lord Moran, was the Dean. Tim had been his house physician after he qualified. He was a friend of our uncle Godfrey who had allowed him to convert an old mill on his property at Manton to be used as a country cottage for which he paid no rent.

Initially I had digs in Gloucester Terrace but when my old friend of Marlborough days, Terence Milne, came to live in a bed-sitting room in Southwick Street I joined him there. I had kept up with Terence at Cambridge although we were in different colleges and had spent some wonderful holidays with the Milnes in their country holiday home at Treaddur Bay, near Holyhead. Sir James Milne was General Manager of the

Great Western Railway. Terence was working in some electrical company at that time. Almost as soon as I arrived at Mary's Hugh Glanville, an Old Marlburian contemporary of mine who had gone straight to Mary's, sought me out and invited me to meet two of his friends in his digs. I had hardly known Hugh at Marlborough but it was typical of him to perform that kindly act and the two he invited me to meet became very close friends. One, Sandy Mills, has been dead for a good many years; the other, Terry Barwell, although living in Cornwall, I still see regularly, as also Hugh Glanville himself. Hugh spent most of his time tinkering underneath his old car rather than attending to his medical studies and never achieved a University Medical Degree, just MRCS LRCP – this did not prevent him from becoming the European Professor of Physical Medicine with international repute.[1]

When I entered Mary's in 1937 war was becoming increasingly likely. Then came Munich and a short breathing space rudely shattered by the invasion of Austria in the spring of 1939. By August war seemed inevitable and on 1 September Poland was invaded. Preparations had been made for most of the hospital to be evacuated to escape air raids. The patients were sent to sector hospitals in the country under the broad jurisdiction and control of the St Mary's consultants; we students were also sent to the sector hospitals. Some went to Hillingdon, Edgware and Amersham; many of us were told to go to Park Prewett Hospital just outside Basingstoke which we shared with

---

[1] He was to receive a large number of honorary degrees – none by examinations.

21

St Thomas's Hospital. After spending the day of 1 September, a Friday, in the Mary's maternity department I suggested to one of my student friends who had a car that he joined me for the weekend at Marlborough before reporting to Park Prewett on the Monday. David Howell and I drove down to Marlborough late in the evening – it was already dark when we left London on the first night of the blackout; no street lamps, curtains had to be drawn and lined with black material and cars had special slats over the headlights. It was a strange sensation driving out of London in the dark and down the A4 to Marlborough. On Saturday we helped to convert the Children's Convalescent Home into a War Emergency Hospital. On Sunday morning we heard Neville Chamberlain telling us over the wireless that we were at war with Germany and then continued our work at the Children's Home where ambulances were already arriving with blind evacuees from London; it was expected that London would be subjected to heavy bombing during the first few days of the War.

The following day David drove me to Park Prewett Hospital. This was a large mental hospital just outside Basingstoke, the majority of its inmates had been accommodated elsewhere and the wards were open to receive sick evacuees from London. In fact not many arrived and our time was spent attending lectures by the equally bored consultants and the rather fruitless pastime, anyway initially, of digging trenches in the grounds. I believe it was to improve Hospital drainage. My old friend from nursery days at Marlborough,

Lawrence Bussell, was also a medical student at Mary's after doing his preclinical work at Oxford. He was a keen countryman and had an old horse-drawn caravan which had been in his family for many years. He obtained permission from a local farmer to park this on a field about two miles from the hospital by the Newbury road. I was a keen camper and so I collected my tent from home and pitched it alongside his caravan. We remained there for over two months, cycling down to the hospital each morning. This caravan now rests in a field only a quarter of a mile from where I am writing this; I pass it frequently. This was the time of the phoney war – the hospital remained virtually empty and there was little for us students to do, and so toward the end of the year we returned to Mary's and I to my lodgings in Southwick Street.

Early spring of the next year, 1940, saw the invasion of Norway by the Germans and then the invasion of Belgium, the advance into France and the British evacuation from Dunkirk and the Battle of Britain. Meanwhile I had begun wrestling with my finals; I expect they made allowances for I was always successful. My first was in June when I sat my midwifery. The Battle of Britain was getting well under way and even over London one could sometimes see planes fighting in the sky, all very exciting. At least Churchill had taken control and his oratory did something to reassure us. During August the bombing of London began, initially the docks area. I used to write home regularly and from September my mother kept many of my letters. Unfortunately I usually headed these letters simply with the day of the week and no date – I had not thought of them having a place in posterity! However with the help of my mother's diaries which she wrote each day, my own memory and the occasional one that is dated I hope I have got them more or less in the right order and correctly dated. The first one was written from Southwick Street and is headed Wednesday which I believe makes it 4 September.

> I hope I may be able to get away on Saturday for a couple of nights, in which case I shall catch the 12.30 or some equivalent train. I shall, if I come, bring as many of my possessions as I can, the less one has in London the better these days! We are still having amazingly few casualties, only ten last night, but the damage to property is really becoming pretty terrific. I have not been out but am told it is an awful job getting through the streets.
>
> All the South London stations are closed. I know Guys, the West London and Thomas's have all had to pack up with bombs and I believe Middlesex is in the same boat. Most of us were up from 12.00 to 3 or 4 a.m. last night, very useful from the point of view of war surgery. The teaching here for surgery is still admirable although we never see civilian cases other than raid casualties now, but it is awfully difficult to do any reading.
>
> Everybody remains completely cheerful if a little tired, this is certainly an experience well worth having but one would like to have some idea of what is going to happen next. For goodness sake don't get worried if

I do not turn up on Saturday, I shall have no means of letting you know if I cannot come as the telegraph services are so bad and may very probably be unable to get away.

P.S. Something over 400 bombs dropped on Paddington Borough up to yesterday and only 13 persons killed!

My mother's diary tells me that I did manage to send a telegram and caught a train arriving at Hungerford at 9.38. I returned to London on Sunday evening and wrote about my experiences on the afternoon of the following day, 9 September.

Last night was a most interesting experience, but likely to pall with repetition. The surprising thing is how little frightening it is at present, but I admit I became a bit unhappy about 4 p.m. We got into a raid just before Reading and crept up to Town after that. I suppose it was about Slough that the glow of London became visible, no lights in the train and so we could look out of the windows. Except for the flicker it might have been London before the war.

We reached London about 9.30, no taxis so I had to carry the whole blooming lot to Southwick Street. The bombing was fairly distant and the streets as light as day almost which was a help. I went round to the Hospital and arranged to move in, which I did about 12.0. I slept with a friend in someones sitting room on the camp bed, or rather lay down there. About 3.0 a gas warning came through, luckily my mask was in the Medical School. I need hardly say a false alarm only, I never expected anything else. About 4.0 things got a bit close, I don't mind the noise or the planes or the fires but object to hearing the bomb 10 seconds before it arrives. We most of us congregated down stairs, but believe it or not only one case came in all night, and that a woman who had hysterics in a shelter. The All Clear went at about 6 a.m. & then I got some sleep. A thunder storm added to the chaos during the night, four balloons were struck by lightning! I went to the roof this morning imagining I should see a devastated London, but except for a few patches of smoke it appeared absolutely normal. The nearest big damage was a cinema beside Madam Tussauds, & to a certain extent Madam Tussauds itself. We have had some cases brought in this afternoon from a block of flats round there.

I am afraid St. Thomas's was hit last night, 5 people missing there but otherwise all right. There is no doubt the noise is out of all proportion to the damage here in the West, it is not pleasant but will be got used to. Posts are a bit disorganised, a P.C. from Daddy thanking me for my letter arrived this evening.

I cannot think what we are all going to do over our examinations, it really is well nigh impossible to work at all. Tonight I shall sleep somewhere in a basement, but I can assure you the chances of being injured are incredibly remote.

P.S. Mrs Drake most grateful for everything, lettuces apparently unobtainable in London.

Mrs Drake was my landlady at Southwick Street; she had a living-in domestic named Ebba. The 'blooming lot' included my camp bed.

On Thursday, 12 September (this letter is dated) I

wrote a long letter to Tim which I typed (on my portable) and was written in St Mary's. Tim being familiar with the hospital I thought he would like to know what was happening. Handfield-Jones was the senior surgeon, Hope Gosse the senior physician, Frazer was a lecturer in physiology, young, gifted and good company. Professor Fleming hardly needs any introduction.

This is terrific, London really is worth living in these days! We have had our ups and downs this week and after last night are having a terrific up. Tuesday was pretty awful, I must own to having been very badly frightened at times, it is pretty awful to hear these things come whistling down at you, but with our A.A. barrage last night we feel grand again, everybody is going about this morning with cheerful faces. [On 11 September a large number of AA guns were moved in to London; this was the first night we had heard our guns answering back.]

When I wrote home last Tuesday I talked about moving in to the basement of the Inoculation Dept. that night, but someone suddenly started a rumour they had a lot of cholera germs down there and we thought better of it. Instead I began with two friends in one of the ground floor sitting rooms, but it began to get a bit unhealthy and we decamped to the passage. Bombing was pretty continuous and there was no A.A. fire at all, they seemed to do just as they pleased. One big one landed at the junction of Harrow and Edgeware Road and another at the Marble Arch, and there were many more all round. Still very few cases, though what there were were rather nasty. They brought in a 3 months old baby which had been dug out of a house and was quite unhurt, the mother had been treated for minor injuries previously. At about 3 a.m. I was called to hold down a shell shocked soldier in Almoth Wright [a ward on the top floor of the hospital]. It really was not too nice up there. Every time we heard a plane come it began to drop bombs, and every time explosions started this poor devil tried to get out of bed. He was pretty doped with morphia and so fairly easy to handle. When the explosions got very close or we heard the scream of a bomb the nurses got under the table and I half under the bed with one hand clutching on to the soldier to hold him down! However I induced him to take some paraldehyde after about two hours and then left him.

The nurses are really marvellous, they have to stay up in those few wards that have any patients and are amazingly cool. None of us really slept before the all clear on Tuesday night, lack of sleep is one of the chief troubles for all.

There were a few odd raids yesterday, the guns in Hyde Park shot down a Messerschmidt over the Old Kent Road. Then about 8.30 the evening raid started, and the guns. [This was the first night of the AA barrage – the guns had been moved into London the previous day.] There never was a more pleasant sound, they are marvellous and are everywhere. Some of them are mobile, there were some of them actually firing in Southwick Crescent, Ebba picked up a great shell cap on the door step this morning. The shrapnel comes down like hail, great big lumps weighing 3 and 4 pounds, there never was such music.

We are at last becoming organised at the hospital and

spent last night in the Inoculation Dept. basement. We included a whole lot of students and residents and Hope Gosse who has come in principally for company I think. King and Cokkinis also sleep now in the hospital corridors. The A.A. fire prevented the bombing being so widespread as the previous night, but they demolished a cinema at the beginning of the Harrow Road and a furniture warehouse between the hospital and Edgeware Road.

The Hospital Home Guard composed of junior students were properly in action for the first time. Their job is to man all departments of the Hospital, Medical School and Nurses Home. They have watchers on the roof, a proceeding which calls for great courage, quite seriously, as it involves throwing oneself flat on one's face at intervals of 10 minutes or so. That perhaps is an exaggeration, but quite often enough anyway. Last night's A.A. fire finished that, the shrapnel proved too much for everyone, but they still have to be up at the top to see where incendiaries drop, and they are going to have a little block house built on the roof. Anyway to get back to last night. An incendiary bomb landed in South Wharf Road, or rather on a building on the far side of it, just by Sabey's Yard. Immediately those down below were informed by telephone and headed by Frazer they made a dash for the building. Frazer seized the first thing he could find to smash down the door and get in, he achieved his object and one of the H.G. bolted in and mounted the stairs followed by Frazer who was still carrying his battering ram. It was in fact a fire extinguisher which had been lying by the door, and the fellow in front of him was getting the full force of its contents on the seat of his trousers! As it was acid he is a bit uncomfortable today.

They found the roof blazing hard and set to work on it, and within about 5 minutes the London Fire Brigade were in action and the blaze got under control. It is vital to get these fires out at once as they are followed by high explosives, also this fire adjoined a petrol pump.

One cannot speak too highly of the fire fighters and A.R.P. people in general. The whole place is lit up by fires all round at times, and yet they are got under control at staggering speed.

I do wish you could have seen Hope Gosse arriving at the hospital yesterday, I don't know why but it really was an amazingly funny spectacle. He was driven up in his large car by his chauffeur and emerged from it with a suit case while the chauffeur followed carrying a spring mattress and bedding, and the two of them descended into the Inoculation Department. I gather Professor Fleming is to join us there tonight. When I came across to the hospital this morning at 8.30 I saw a sorry procession wending its way into the hospital headed by Miss Cass [Ophthalmic Dept.], they had a time bomb in the block of flats in which she lives.

I have not ventured down to the West End at all, indeed I have been too busy, but a number of streets round Piccadilly are closed, the Burlington Arcade is smashed and they had a time bomb which went off in Regent Street yesterday afternoon. All the windows in the Examination Hall are broken, but I understand the exams are to be held in London all right. H-J [Handfield-Jones] said yesterday he heard if a warning went during the written exam the papers would be scrapped and we would have vivas and clinical only. Of

30

course it is fantastic to do any reading, and really the whole exam is going to be farcical, I do not see how they will deal with the matter. I will say one thing, surgical teaching is proceeding quite normally, except of course for rounds as there are practically no patients. Also it is considered a gala day if we get one new out patient coming up. It all has to be theoretical.

Well, I am afraid this letter is very badly written, but I hope it gives you some idea of life in London, which believe me is very exciting. There was a bomb yesterday afternoon between Paddington and Ealing and the line was closed completely for some hours, but I think it is just working today and hope you will get this letter in due course. Anyway we are all very happy up here.

There follows a PS written in my own hand.

Just one more story. Someone told me today when they turned on the gas in his house they had a spurt of water. Gas pressure is very low everywhere, most cooking has to be done on paraffin. Ebba is taking all this very calmly, and Mrs Drake for that matter. I do think people are standing up to it awfully well so far. They told me they never laughed so much as they did on Tuesday night. Please tell family I will write again in a few days, also I am going to leave Southwick St. completely & will get my keep at the Hospital.

I wrote home quite frequently during this time despite pressure of trying to prepare for my surgical finals. The following is extracted from a letter which I believe must have been written on 13 September; it was just headed Sunday. Sir G-L was Sir Ernest

Graham-Little, a dermatologist who had become an MP. All MPs had been issued with tin hats but as he had evacuated himself to the Ailesbury Arms Hotel in Marlborough – Parliament was not sitting anyway in London – he kindly passed his hat on to me.

I have collected up Sir G-L's tin hat, 103 are on order by the hospital but it may be ages before we get them and in the meantime this is most useful. Actually one does not venture out much at night now anyway, shrapnel comes down like rain, great lumps of it. The A.A. barrage really is terrific, most comforting! I have not heard a bomb close for days now, the A.A. fire masks the sounds so.

A real thrill this morning. I was packing up in Southwick St. when the sirens went, one takes no notice of them during the day now, and having finished there was returning to the hospital. As I crossed Hyde Park Crescent I heard terrific machine gun fire just above. I went on a bit further and joined some friends in a doorway. The sky was patchy with clouds, but there were a good many clear places. We could hear the roar of planes & machine gunning, and then suddenly a bomber emerged, quite low really, and fighters buzzing round it like wasps. Even as we watched an airman bailed out and next moment the bomber went into a cloud and then reappeared nose diving into the ground, it must have landed in Victoria direction some way away, possibly South of the river. Two minutes later another huge bomber came crashing down rather closer, it might have been in Hyde Park.

The streets were packed with people, all up from their basements, and everybody was cheering like blazes. It really was terrific, a most heartening sight for all Londoners.

On the whole London is much less damaged than one might expect, but it is a bit trying getting about as so many streets are roped off with time bombs. I tried to get to Lewis's library to change a book yesterday morning, but it was closed with an unexploded bomb. Today I have been having lunch and tea with Terence & Virginia. [Terence Milne had married two years previously – he was in a reserved occupation.] A stick of bombs has straddled their flat but none close enough to break the windows, they were very lucky. I was getting close to Buckingham Palace yesterday morning on my bicycle when the sirens went and thought better of it and beat a hasty retreat! I wish you could see London now, I believe most people outside would be pleasantly surprised by the lack of damage. Anyway since Wednesday and the A.A. fire everybody is perfectly cheerful here, and if truth be known I believe people are rather enjoying the excitement.

P.S. I seem to have written a whole letter without mentioning invasion, but then one does rather live from day to day up here. Personally I still doubt if they can attempt it.

There is no doubt the morale of Londoners during this time was fantastic. Everyone pulled together and the community spirit had to be experienced to be believed. It was particularly noticeable in the Hospital where consultants, junior doctors and students were all thrown together day and night. Handfield-Jones – the surgeon – used to give us tutorials in the evenings in one of the resident's rooms on the ground floor; I remember once we all dived under the table round which we were sitting when a bomb fell uncomfortably close.

A favourite place to foregather was the Fountains, a pub just across the other side of Praed Street from which the porters from the hospital could extract anyone who was on duty and was required. Professor Fleming had joined us in our basement dormitory and was a regular imbiber at the Fountains. André Maurois in his biography of Fleming refers to this and his liking for his 'pot of beer'. Although we knew about penicillin, it was not then available; we did not even know that Florey and Chain were working on it at Oxford. Fleming was not a good lecturer but a likeable man who seemed to enjoy our company and the convivial atmosphere of the Fountains. I remember him so well, always with a cigarette dangling from his lips. On occasion he would invite one or two of us up to his laboratory to drink sherry out of beakers. He once asked me why none of the Maurices were Freemasons (he was a dedicated Mason himself); I was able to tell him that in fact my father was a Mason – not I believe a very keen one. I wondered if he was hinting I might become one myself.

During this time, which was the height of the Blitz, I wrote home with great frequency even though I sometimes managed to escape to Marlborough for the weekend. I actually did write the date on the letter I wrote on 17 September.

Another letter from you this morning, posts to Marlborough seem better than to most other places.

Paddington has come off very lightly so far, nothing more than an occasional time bomb on the line. I don't think we have had any special excitements since I last wrote, we had a rather specially heavy raid last night which shook the buildings about a bit, but casualties are still almost negligible. We only had 6 last night, all from Marylebone which was hit just as a train came in, none of them in the least serious.

It is quite an adventure getting round London now. Personally I always use a bicycle on those rare occasions when I do go out, one of which was this morning. I wanted to get to the Strand and had to make three or four detours going through Mayfair, there was a lot doing in that direction last night. The Strand itself has an enormous crater in the middle of the road. I came back via Buckingham Palace, the main front looks much as usual except for a few broken panes and one crater where the front railings were [all iron railings had been removed and sent to armament factories]. Park Lane was closed and all traffic had to go through the park. I cannot imagine what the winter will be like in this place, if we continue as at present all movement will be restricted to about six or eight hours while it is light.

It is queer how completely we have adjusted to these new conditions, I think I have slept better than I do in normal times this last week. The only difficulty is concentration, I tried my uttermost to work after the raid had begun at 8 p.m. last night but found it a complete impossibility with all the racket going on all round. But sleep does come easily, I shall have to get someone to soothe me to sleep banging trays about outside my door when next I come home!

The restaurant staff are magnificent here. They have all had their fair share of being bombed and yet we get very good meals very well served. Last night two of them could not get back to their homes as the raid began extra early, awful for them as they had children there, and so I think in future we are going to have a high tea and so let them off early. The Manageress, who is very efficient, had been to visit her home and was coming back as she sleeps in the hospital. However the raid started early and the bus stopped so she spent the night in the Paddington Police Station! Communications are getting increasingly difficult, the telephone works only spasmodically even to such places as Hampstead now. One man told me he came up from Southampton yesterday and was pushed out at Wimbledon from which he was shepherded by devious routes until after about two hours he arrived at the Elephant & Castle, and he wanted to get to Paddington!

Could you please send me a towel, the hospital ones are so very small? Otherwise I think I am fairly well supplied. It is certainly absurd of Uncle Henry & Aunt Ruth to stay in Town, everyone who can go out should be made to as it so much easier for the rest.

My mother's diary does show that my uncle and aunt did indeed evacuate themselves to Marlborough the weekend after I wrote that letter and I also spent Saturday and Sunday nights at home, returning on Monday, 23 September. I wrote again on Wednesday the 25th. Lancelot Creyke referred to was my Aunt Sylvia's brother.

We had a very good run up on Monday & got to the hospital by 11.0 which was when I wanted to be there.

We arrived during a raid & could see smoke spirals made by fighting planes in the sky but nothing more.

Mrs Drake was most grateful for the flowers & vegetables. They had an incendiary bomb through the roof on Saturday night at Southwick St. It became lodged by a water tank and did not get right through to the bathroom floor below. Ebba smelt burning & rushed up stairs & found it & then called the wardens & they got it out with two stirrup pumps. The house on the other side of the road was not so lucky, it was empty and the two top floors were badly burned.

Most of us here are up for Finals & making great effort to do some work, but it really is hard after dark. Last night a friend of mine & I worked for an hour & on 4 occasions we had to rush out of the room & throw ourselves flat on our faces in the passage outside! There was quite a haze from cordite in the hospital by 10 p.m., the bombs were dropped just outside Paddington Station. At 4 a.m. we were all woken up by terrific explosions which broke some glass in the wards and now abandoned operating theatres. Again not more than a dozen casualties all told.

Is Walter Creyke really Lancelot Creyke or his brother? He was brought in here on Monday night having got involved with a tube train; the story I heard was he sat on the platform and dangled his legs over the edge as the train came in! He will be all right but is in rather a mess. He asked if anyone knew the Maurices? I saw him today but he was asleep, but I did not think he was Lancelot.

There follows the greater part of a letter I wrote home on 28 September. Godfrey Wynne was very much a downmarket journalist, a rather precious looking little man, but his comments on town hall bureaucracy which could exist at the height of the London Blitz make interesting reading.

Thank you for your letter which came this morning. I did not think he was Lancelot Creyke when I saw him, but he was fairly bad and I did not say who I was; people look so much older when they are ill. He has now been transferred to Harefield Hospital, Middlesex. [He was indeed Lancelot Creyke, and he died from his injuries.] We had a fairly eventful night on Thursday. In the first place that horrid little man Godfrey Wynne, late of the *Daily Mirror* and now of the *Sunday Express* spent the night in the Hospital. He improves slightly on closer acquaintance and even made himself useful helping to carry a dead man to the mortuary.

At about 10 p.m. the alarms rang which means there is trouble about and I went over to the Hospital from the Inoculation Dept. to see what was up. There was a very big fire raging just across the road in Paddington Wharf, or to be exact several big fires. Flames were leaping up and the whole place was as light as day. I was watching it with two residents from a bathroom window when a stick of H.E.'s were dropped. We heard the bombs coming and I do not think the three of us have ever moved so fast before. We made a concerted dive along a passage and colliding with a swing door all fell on top of each other in a heap. Usually I am first in these rushes, but this time I was last and fell on top of the others, for which I was heartily thankful, it was a stone floor!

I then went to the residents dining room where most

of the personnel of the Hospital were gathered. Almost I was sorry for Godfrey Wynne. The arch humorist of the students had been turned on to him and his leg was being pulled so badly I almost thought it would come right off! Everybody else was sitting round roaring with laughter at him.

When we got out from there we found the Hospital had been burning quite nicely above our heads. However our Home Guard of students soon had the fires out, I cannot think where we should be without them. The biggest fire was in Mitchell Bird, a ward close to the roof. The H.G. really are immensely efficient, I am sure they stopped what would have been a really serious fire on this occasion.

It was then decided to shift all the patients to the basement, there were about 50 of them. We got them all down fairly quickly but it was rather a job, the lifts would not take the beds as they, the lifts, were too small. We again had very few casualties, about a dozen, and except for one who was dead comparatively minor.

Wynne was quite interesting on the subject of East London where he had spent 3 nights and days. After that he wrote an article, it was the first time for about 15 years he has had one refused, only Beaverbrook being in the Government makes the *Express* careful in what it says. To give one example of what he found. Those who are homeless have to go to the Town Hall to fill up a form, Form E, which entitles them to get accommodation from the Government. They soon ran out of form E's and so a clerk went down the queue, which ran for hundred of yards, telling them they must leave their names and addresses and form E's would be sent to them by post to fill up at home, I ask you, their addresses! He also said they build brick shelters without roofs, he was told they were short of concrete!

The tube stations all over London are packed with people by 4 p.m. now, a pathetic spectacle, the disease is going to be appalling. I believe it will be physicians, not surgeons, we shall want in this war. Incidentally I have now been inoculated against flu, colds and meningitis, in addition to typhoid, paratyphoid, cholera, tetanus and diphtheria.

We only had about 19 patients in the Hospital last night, all the rest having been sent out. At last the authorities are getting alive to the situation. Handfield-Jones has come to live in, and he is one of the few people in the place who do not mind telling people to go to the devil! I understand he is beginning on the Dean, with the Chairman of the Board of Governors a good second. Dickson-Wright [a surgeon of great standing] turned up on Thursday night, an H.E. exploded 25 yards from him and blew him over just beside his house, and a time bomb in the house next door forced him to leave. Professor Fleming and Dr. Hope Gosse have had incendiaries in their houses and quite a number of students have had their houses demolished. However London looks fairly normal by day, though damage is fairly easy to find.

A letter from the laundry tells us that the whole place was completely destroyed. They were unable to write before as the office and stationary was included in the destruction. I luckily had only a few things there, as I think I said before, but Mrs Drake lost a lot. We had a lot of raids yesterday, a terrific barrage was put up on 2 occasions, unusual by day.

My exam on Wednesday, heaven knows what it will

be like, I have tried to work but it really is well nigh impossible in these conditions. However they are bound to make allowances. Anyway I have never bothered so little about an exam before, but I do not know if that will help or not.

In these letters I wrote home I do not mention how we were able to deal with casualties when the operating theatres, which were on the top floor of the Hospital were closed. A large ward on the ground floor of the Hospital was used for surgery. There were about six operating tables and the surgeons and registrars assisted by us senior students carried out whatever was necessary on the casualties. Although I was stressing in my letters that we were getting relatively few casualties there were often three or four teams operating simultaneously.

I duly cycled to Queen's Square to sit my final conjoint board examination in surgery on Wednesday, 2 October. Several streets were blocked and I had to make more than one detour. I duly wrote home that evening:

I have the usual post-examination depression! I would not have minded so much if it had been a paper which I couldn't do, but there was nothing in it really that I couldn't have done all right if I had used my wits properly.

The sirens have been wailing continuously all day including during the exam, which was also punctuated by explosions, but only time bombs I imagine [I do remember there was virtually no glass in the

41

examination hall windows which just had paper covering them]. Those up for medicine this morning heard a dog fight going on above their heads!

Your letter came this morning. I had heard that Lancelot Creyke had died, he had been getting much better and it was not really expected when he left here. Either we are now quite acclimatised to London's night life or things have been very much quieter here lately. I think I may try to get a few days holiday after this exam pass or fail, I certainly could do with one.

P.S. Please send cheque, suggest £10.

The written exam was followed some days later by a viva and clinical examination; I remember little about either. Anyway the examiners were merciful and I duly passed although the news of our results were not published until 11 October. I had spent the previous Saturday night at home and as soon as I heard I had been successful I caught a train home, getting to Marlborough about 8.30 p.m. I then had a whole week's relaxation and did not return to London until the following Friday, 18 October. I wrote home the following day, having caught a train which had left Swindon at 4.05 p.m.

My journey up was pretty bad. We were supposed to get to Paddington at 5.42 but were still in Reading at 6.42. Why it should have been quite as late as it was I never discovered, we seemed to go quicker after Reading than before in spite of the evening raid which we ran into at West Drayton. A raid means all the lights in the train are put out and so the curtains and blinds can be drawn giving a good view out, but there was little to see beyond gun flashes. We eventually got in about 8, a four hour journey!

It was too late to get any food at the Hospital and so I left my things there and went back to Paddington Hotel grill with a friend who drank some coffee and was able to tell me all the news. This particular friend, one Binkie Pattrick, being quite without fear has been sleeping all these weeks in Norfolk Square on the top floor of a lodging house. When they dropped something that seems to have been a mixture between an H.E. and a land mine in the Square early this week it blew all his glass in and the contents of his wardrobe onto the floor. He dressed and went out and a man asked for help in getting some people out of the basement of a nearby house which had been destroyed. They got into the basement with great difficulty but could not locate the people in it in spite of the noise they were making. However he went back to the Hospital and got some morphia and ultimately sufficient of each person was found to inject some morphia and so get them quiet and remove them.

That same night a block of flats was demolished in which I have several friends. One man who had a flat there was Dr. Maclean who is a bacteriologist here and whom I know well. He had been out all day and was just making his bed, he was tucking in the foot when a block of masonry landed on the pillow. He put out a hand at a wall which was coming toward him and the wall split into three parts, the piece his hand was on remained still and the other parts went past on either side. The only damage he suffered was a broken leg, and that was a tin one, a relic of the last war, and he got it repaired the next day!

43

The Paddington area has indeed changed very considerably for the worse since I was last here. Amazing that the line and station are all right. Norfolk Sq. has no houses right down, but not a single house is usable in the half adjoining Norfolk Place and there are quite honestly not more than about half a dozen whole panes of glass anywhere in the Square. 16 Southwick St. is all right except that there is no glass anywhere in the back of the house, a small H.E. dropped two doors away. Mrs Drake and Ebba seem quite happy and Mrs D. most grateful for the flowers and fruit.

For the first three nights of this week no one seems to have had more than an hour's sleep a night. On Sunday they had 3 tables in the theatre for nearly 12 hours continuously, but not more than 50 cases all told. Since Wednesday things have been much quieter. This afternoon I went with a friend from Westminster Pier to Wapping by water bus. It costs the great sum of three pence, and involves changing into a tug for the latter half of the journey. Of course things were pretty bad, but again nothing like so bad as I had expected. The most striking thing was the dreadful emptiness of the place, hardly a man to be seen anywhere. Wapping did not smell very nice either, and I had no idea all the notices down there were printed in Yiddish. We came back by bus. On the way down we had a raid and some planes flew over, not very high. Guns got into action from the banks and I must say I put on my tin hat!

Coming back we had some excitement too. We heard the steady hooting of a car in the distance getting closer. Everyone in the street got out of the way and then a car came down the road going hell for leather past traffic lights and all. It flashed past us and disappeared round a corner, and on it in large letters was BOMB DISPOSAL. Oh gosh!!

I rang up Mr Williamson at Bromley tonight and got straight through. I am lunching there tomorrow if I can get to Bromley & so will continue this letter tomorrow evening. Before I forget – St. Margarets, Westminster does not look at all badly damaged, a few burned pews lying outside – but otherwise it seems quite normal.

Sunday. A quietish night, quieter anyway than I had expected because it was very clear. However, we were a little riled this morning when a warning went just after breakfast and a minute later a stick of bombs came down, three on one side and one on the other of the Hospital. [Forty-eight years later I know exactly where I was sitting when we were straddled by those bombs, on the loo in the medical school! It had an excellent cathartic effect.]

It was a glorious day today, and having found the Bromley North line was closed I decided to bicycle. It is quite a pleasant run and took only 1½ hours in spite of diversions. I was really surprised at the smallness of the damage all the way down.

The Williamsons seemed fairly well and had Dick home for the week-end, he is now at Cheltenham & Ken & wife at Hereford. They have reinforced a room on the ground floor and put up a brick wall outside the window as protection from blast. Mr W motors up to Town each day & neither have been away at all. I think they might manage to get away for a long week-end but they hadn't liked to suggest your taking them. They are both obviously very tired, and as there are large guns just outside the house the noise is deafening, indeed they have an enormous crack across the house caused by shaking from the guns.

I think they might possibly come next weekend if you could have them, and as Mr W has a meeting in Guildford on Thursday they might motor on from there. Since Uncle Henry will have gone Mr W could presumably sleep up there. I don't know how you feel about having them so soon, but suggest that you write or ring them up, the phone usually works. They have had several land mines round and one is apt to be machine gunned on the golf course. Bombs were dropped quite close while I was there & we retired from the garden to the house for a time. I made an uneventful return by train this evening. Sorry this letter is so long, not much paper economy I am afraid.

Very sadly Dick Williamson was tragically killed a little later in the War. Ken & Jim, the other brother, will appear later in these pages. My parents were good hosts to a large number of friends and relations who had either suffered bomb damage or who just needed to escape for a time from the turmoil in which they were living; this was in addition to the five City of London School boys evacuated to Marlborough and sleeping in Lloran House.

On 27 October I was able to write home that there was much less night bombing and that I had been able to do more work preparing for my final exam, the LRCP, than in the previous five weeks. 'The only night we had any trouble was Tuesday when an oil bomb landed on Whiteleys where a lot of people were sheltering. I was up until 6.30 treating burns, many of them very bad I fear. By day a single plane has been apt to get in and release a few bombs but it has not been at all bad really.' I also commented in this letter that I was glad the Williamsons had managed to get down for a long weekend.

During November things remained very much quieter and I have no letters written then or indeed until after I had joined the Army in 1942; but I do have some memories and my mother's scribbled diaries. I came home for Christmas on Tuesday, 24 December and returned to London the following Sunday, 29 December. I have vivid memories of arriving at Paddington – it was the night the Germans launched their great fire raid on the City of London. It might almost have been daylight as I walked up Praed Street to the Hospital. I went up to the roof to see the conflagration, an incredible spectacle still etched in my memory.

My written papers were on 1 January followed shortly after by the vivas and clinicals and at last I was a qualified doctor. There was no compulsory pre-registration in those days – we went straight on the medical register. However we were permitted to do a year of resident jobs in hospitals before being called up into the forces. I applied to be House Physician to Dr Hope Gosse, the senior Consultant Physician at St Mary's and duly obtained the post. The Germans were turning their attention now to the provincial cities, Coventry, Liverpool, Portsmouth, Plymouth etc. and London was comparatively quiet. The medical wards were kept open and in action and I was able to get quite good experience. During my six months at Mary's we did have two very heavy raids, the first on 16 April and the second on 10 May. Fortunately St Mary's escaped but none of us had any sleep on those nights.

With reduced beds there were only two medical firms in the Hospital at this time, Hope Gosse's and Professor Pickering's. He was later to become Sir George, Regius Professor of Medicine at Oxford and then Master of Pembroke College, Oxford. His HP, newly qualified like me, was Dick Lovell who was later to become Professor of Medicine at Melbourne University. Hope Gosse was primarily a chest physician and was also physician at the Brompton Hospital; he kindly came down and proposed our health when Anne and I married in Marlborough in 1947. In addition to Hope Gosse I was also HP to Dr Wilfred Harris, the Neurologist, who also had a few in-patients. For some reason he and Hope Gosse were not on speaking terms, something to do with a road accident when Wilfred Harris was driving, and so any communication between them had to be passed through me. Sir William Willcox, a very senior Physician, was also called out of retirement and would see patients from time to time. I was always warned of his impending visits when he would be driven up to the front door of the Hospital in Praed Street, no side entrance for him. I would be standing on the steps to receive him as his Rolls Royce drew up at the entrance and solemnly escort him to the ward where he would duly examine one or two patients and pronounce his opinion on them. Dick Lovell and I also had to take our turn in the Casualty Department where a variety of cases came our way. Many of the attenders were living under horrific conditions due to the Blitz; their cheerfulness and high morale never ceased to amaze me.

I enjoyed my time as House Physician at St Mary's enormously and was sorry when it came to an end on 30 June. We residents who were leaving the Hospital had been thrown together and had come to know our chiefs in a way which could never be possible except under conditions of war. There were four of us and we decided to wine and dine our respective chiefs, George Pickering, Hope Gosse, Handfield-Jones and Douglas Macleod, the Gynaecologist. The Registrars with whom we had formed excellent relationships were invited too for good measure. We started in a pub with a few beers and then repaired to a restaurant in the basement underneath the old Criterion restaurant at Piccadilly Circus, which could always be relied on to give quite a good meal despite the rationing. We then moved on to a pub at Hyde Park Corner much frequented by students and doctors from St George's Hospital which was located on the Corner at that time. At closing time six of us somehow squeezed into a little Hillman Minx belonging to Handfield-Jones to be driven back to St Mary's. In those days the road through Hyde Park to Marble Arch was two-way with road islands at intervals; one of these got out of control and hit us; we skidded across into the pavement on the wrong side of the road. We all scrambled out and then saw a burly policeman advancing on us through the fading light, double summer time in those war years. My chief exclaimed, 'Ooh Ooh, the cops,' and lit out for Mayfair, closely followed by his loyal House Physician. Handfield-Jones, as we afterwards heard, went up to the policeman and said, 'I am Mishter Handfield-Jonesh of Sht Mary's Hoshpital – and here's two poundsh.' He then drove back to the Hospital where we all foregathered later – well – there was a war on.

In July I went to one of the St Mary's sector hospitals at Amersham to be House Surgeon to Brian King. The hospital was an old workhouse with huts built in the grounds. I also had charge of the ENT beds under Mr Livingstone who was consultant at the Radcliffe Infirmary and lived in Oxford. He had removed a number of tonsils that day and no sooner had I arrived than two of the children began to bleed heavily. I could not contact Mr Livingstone and so all I could do was to transfuse them, grouping and cross matching myself – it was before the days of the rhesus factor. Luckily they both survived. Amersham was a restful time after London although the work was demanding and there was little time for recreation. House Surgeons had to accept much greater responsibility than they do today but it was all good experience although not always to the advantage of the patients.

In the first two weeks of August I was given leave. A party of senior boys from Marlborough College were going to Scotland to do some forestry work on the Duke of Buccleugh's estate at Drumlanrig, led by my old housemaster, G. Kempson. G and I had become

50

friends, indeed I had been best man at his wedding before the War, and he suggested I too might join the party; perhaps he thought my novice medical knowledge would not come amiss. I remember the journey on the night mail from Euston well. The train was crowded with troops going on leave and we had difficulty even in sitting down. After an uncomfortable night we arrived unwashed and unshaven at Thornhill station where we were met by a chauffeur with a large estate car and driven straight to Drumlanrig Castle where we were ushered into breakfast with the Duke and Duchess of Buccleugh. In fact they could not have been more charming and after breakfast and a wash the Duke drove us in his car round his estate. I well remember how impressed I was by his knowledge of what exactly was going on in the various areas we visited. Next day the rest of the party arrived and we got down to our forestry work. I should say we were accommodated quite comfortably in the stable block which included a bathroom and all modern conveniences.

My other memory of our stay there was the arrival of the Duke and Duchess of Gloucester. The Duke was King George's brother and the Duchess was the sister of the Duke of Buccleugh. The first intimation we had of their arrival was the delivery of the Royal Standard; it was rumoured that the Duke's dirty washing was wrapped up inside. There was a large drying room (essential in the inevitable wet weather we experienced) in the basement of the castle close to the boiler; I do remember one of our party found he was wearing underpants with H.R.H. embellished on them. One night we were all invited into the castle where we sang songs to the accompaniment of the Duke of Gloucester on a piano.

It was on the day of our return to Marlborough, 14 August 1941, that we heard of the dramatic meeting between Churchill and Roosevelt in Newfoundland and the signing of what they called the 'Declaration of Intent'; at least the Americans were firmly on our side. Back at Amersham life continued on its relatively normal course and I was still there on 7 December when the Japanese unexpectedly, and I suppose literally, out of the blue bombed Pearl Harbour; the Americans had finally been drawn into the War and we knew that ultimately we were bound to win.

CHAPTER IV

The RAMC, 1942

In February 1942 I was called up into the RAMC on completion of my year's resident posts. All doctors became lieutenants with two pips on joining the Army but we had to do a two-week course at Crookham before being posted to a unit. This was rather like being back in the OTC but I suppose we had to be taught how to salute and march, not that doctors had to do much of the latter. It must have been in early March that I received notice of my first posting – I was to join a Field Ambulance Headquarters at Bridestowe – Bridestowe which I knew so well, and less than a mile from where I used to camp with the College scouts on Dartmoor. On arrival there I found the Field Ambulance was accommodated in a lovely Georgian House – Millaton House – which stood in extensive grounds and had been requisitioned from a young Guards officer who had inherited a barony when only twenty – his name was Peter Carrington. I shared a room with one other officer and we had a large bathroom en suite. There was not much work to do and no medicine and I soon began to long for patients.

My mother did not keep any of the letters I had written home until she received one I had written on

1 April. Very surprisingly this did not come from Bridestowe but was headed 'Prince of Wales Hospital, Devonport'. I started my letter by saying how my every wish seemed to get granted – how only the previous day I had written to Lawrence Bussell saying I was homesick for patients and wishing I had some medical work to do. I continued my letter:

By this afternoon I find myself Resident Medical Officer, the only one, in this very pleasant Hospital – a civilian Hospital without a single service patient in it. It is a subsidiary of the big Plymouth Hospital and the Medical Superintendent there has impressed on me that I am in charge of the place although of course there are honorary surgeons for the big surgery. What happened was that the C.O. sent for me this morning about 11 o'clock and said that he had been asked to supply someone for the post for a week and wanted me to go. He had never heard of such a thing before and thought it might be the general's idea of an April fool, but I had better go and see. I was accordingly driven over to Plymouth and saw the Medical Superintendent at Plymouth Hospital. The trouble here was that they normally had two residents, one was called up a week ago and the other, a wild Irishman, has made himself so objectionable they have to sack him. I gather he was all right as a doctor but was refusing to see out-patients without extra pay.

When I arrived at the Plymouth Hospital they had still not told him he was to go. I came on round here and found he was at the local theatre – still in the dark. A pleasant situation really, appointed in the place of a man who did not know he was sacked!

I went round the wards, dealt with various minor casualties & when the man returned the secretary, a very good sort of fellow, broke it to him. He does not seem to mind too much, he was off soon anyway, & packed his bag. He is coming back to collect it soon, I suppose I shall meet him then, but he seems to have taken it quite quietly.

This Hospital is equipped to take 200 patients but only normally has 70 or 80 and is a bit below that now. The remaining beds are kept for air raid cases. The amenities of the Hospital, departments like theatre, X-ray & so on are all excellent, well up to the 200 mark. I have got one of the surgeons to come round tomorrow anyway, I gather they would like me to do some surgery myself. So there I am, I still feel as if I might wake up soon but it seems to be true. Incidentally there is a naval M.O. who comes to give a hand in the morning if I want to go out or sees out-patients when I am in the theatre.

P.S. O'Reilly, the wild Irishman, has just been in. He takes it all quite calmly and has been quite useful in giving me some of the ropes about this place. I think I am going to have a good week, grand to have a children's ward again, and it is a very nice one too. Turn-over is very rapid, operation cases sent to other hospitals on the 4th day, that is what keeps the numbers down. I only wish I could stay here a bit longer.

One week later, Wednesday, 8 April, I wrote to say an unwilling Army had extended my stay at Devonport by a further forty-eight hours until my replacement arrived and then I was to go to Drake's Island in

Plymouth Sound to relieve the MO there who was going on leave. However after only two days there someone quite unexpectedly turned up to relieve me and I was then posted to a company of 144th Field Ambulance stationed in an old hotel, The Gables, on the hill above Plympton and four miles out of Plymouth. Initially I was extremely bored with nothing to do after a very hectic ten days. In the course of a long letter I wrote home after I had been there for a week I wrote 'Breakfast 9 a.m., nothing to do till 11 when there is a break for refreshments, 11.30 to 1, nothing, 1-2 lunch, & 2 to 4.30 a repetition of the morning, such is a typical day in the life of an officer in a Field Ambulance.' However by great good fortune my civilian relief at Devonport Hospital was Gordon Barclay. Although I did not positively remember having met him before, we had been at Cambridge at the same time and had a great number of mutual friends. He had recently married a charming girl, Celia. The handover had been a great success and we both agreed that I should help him out at the Hospital when my military duties allowed. This would give him some time off and allow me to keep my hand in.

My period of boredom did not last long and I was soon writing home again with some degree of enthusiasm. It was a long letter written in Devonport Hospital listening to the nine o'clock news and waiting to give someone a blood transfusion. I was very impressed by the comradeship in the company of the Field Ambulance at Plympton. All ranks mucked in together – it was not unusual to see the major, a

56

lieutenant, the staff sergeant and a private having a game of cards together. We numbered some fifty men and three officers. Commandos were all the rage at that time and I was only too happy to devise exercises on boy scout lines to relieve the boredom. In this letter too I described at length some quite large-scale army manoeuvres lasting over two days and nights in which I had been involved. Also I had been appointed relief MO to a battalion of the East Surreys and doing quite a lot of work at Devonport Hospital. Initially the East Surreys treated me with some coldness – they had not liked their previous MO – but I was welcomed with open arms when the second in command suddenly asked me if I was related to the Marlborough Maurices. My cousin Jack – later to be killed and awarded a posthumous DSO at the D-Day landings – was himself a member of the regiment.

I got on well with the major in charge of the Field Ambulance Company but then he got posted away and I found myself in charge of the company. However this was fun. Also I had full use of the company car, a comfortable Humber, which eased the problem of getting to and from Devonport Hospital. In one letter I mention giving an anaesthetic for $2\frac{1}{2}$ hours – I remember the case well – a young man with very severe Crohns disease who had fistulae from the bowel to the bladder.

With the arrival of summer I was determined to do something about the empty swimming pool in the hotel grounds. Various units occupying the hotel had tried to get it filled over the preceding two years without success. An attempt to fill it ourselves nearly ended in our flooding the whole building. I then went to the water authorities and said it was imperative we had a static water tank in our grounds; as the centres of Plymouth and Exeter had been bombed out of existence and raids were still taking place, enough even to shake the Gables, this did not seem unreasonable. They saw my point and the pool was duly filled and my stock rose considerably with the unit.

At the end of June I received a new posting – MO to a battalion of the Buffs stationed near Ivybridge. The battalion commander, Lieutenant Colonel Boucher, was a first-class officer and we got on well. Another officer was Pat Rance with whom I became very friendly; Pat and his wife even came to stay with us in Marlborough after the War. He was to make his name selling French cheeses and now lives in the South of France.[1] My stay with the Buffs was not to be for long – on 8 August I had a weekend at home and then went on a week's course in London on Tropical Medicine. I had been given a week's leave after I had completed the course but while at home I received instructions that my leave was extended to three weeks as I was given embarkation leave. During this time I was able to help out in the practice and then returned to the Buffs only to find another MO had already arrived and so I was granted another ten days leave at home before joining my overseas draft. While in London on my course I had found time to equip myself with a full tropical uniform outfit including the mandatory solar topi.

---

[1] Sadly Pat is now widowed and lives in London.

It was during this final leave extension, 13 September according to my mother's diary, that I went to the Mill Cottage at Manton to say farewell to the Dean of St Mary's, by then Churchill's doctor and Sir Charles Wilson, soon to become Lord Moran. He had just returned with Churchill from North Africa where the C-in-C, General Auchinleck had been relieved of his command. Wilson was full of the trip: 'You see, Dick, morale there was bad – something had to be done – Auchinleck had to go.' There was I with my two 'pips' hearing of the dismissal of a Commander-in-Chief and Wilson almost giving the impression that he was responsible. Sir John Colville in his magnum opus *Fringes of Power – Downing Street Diaries* rather unkindly (as he himself admits) wrote in the biographical notes at the end of the book: 'Lord Moran was never present when history was made, though he was quite often invited to luncheon afterwards.'

It was on 17 September 1942 that, my goodbyes all said, my father drove me to Savernake station to catch the 6.40 p.m. train to Paddington; it was to be three years less just three weeks before I was to see Marlborough again. I spent that night with Terence and Virginia Milne in London and they took me out to dinner at the Berkeley; the following day I travelled by train to Leeds to join Draft RXOZW. My only memory of my stay in Leeds was travelling on a bus to Ilkley Moor and going for a walk there.

CHAPTER V

Passage to India, 1942

On 29 September we embarked on the *Capetown Castle* and sailed out from Liverpool to Belfast Lough where we anchored for a time while the convoy was being collected. My mother kept virtually all the letters I wrote home during my three years abroad but being subject to censorship for much of the time I had to be guarded in what I wrote. However these letters, and I wrote weekly whenever I could, together with my own memory enable me to give some account of my life in the East. Like many of my contemporaries who survived it I can claim to have had a good war – it was an experience I would not have missed for anything. One advantage I had over many: I was used to male society and had never acquired any close friends of the opposite sex, let alone get tied to one; further, I was determined to postpone such ties until after the War and I was home again. Much of what I write will be quotes from my letters. In retrospect I feel almost ashamed of the way in which we officers were treated on our way out to India while the troops undoubtedly had a miserable time; I am glad to say later in the War their conditions did improve and the officers were rather less pampered. The fact that there was no prospect in the near future of posting my letters did not deter me from writing quite frequently on the *Capetown Castle*; the first letter was written shortly after we had sailed.

> The business of getting on board went more smoothly than I had really expected and we seem to be slightly less crowded than I had feared. I have not yet made the acquaintance of all the other four people in my cabin, where incidentally I have secured a very comfortable berth. The cabins are in fact extremely comfortable albeit crowded.
>
> I will of course send you a cable when the opportunity arises, heaven knows when next I will hear from you. We start living absolutely on the fat of the land now. The feeding here is as good as the most expensive London hotels in peace time, there is little else to do but eat really.
>
> I think the voyage really promises to be quite entertaining although I shall be probably extremely glad when it is over and I am able to stretch my legs a bit.
>
> Once again then goodbye.
>
> P.S. It is a strange feeling being able to buy sweets and chocolates without limit, but I am sorry my last words should be dwelling on food. Incidentally I hope that by travelling on this boat I shall be improving your financial situation!

This last quote was to tell my mother I was on a Union Castle Liner, a company in which she had held shares – I knew she had sold them but thought she would get the message – she did!

Our journey south took us far out into the Atlantic to avoid the enemy U-boats. There were many ships in the convoy which at least gave us something to look at and there were a number of destroyers and frigates to accompany us. Depth charges were heard occasionally but the entire convoy got through unscathed.

I penned a letter on 15 October.

> Censorship is fairly heavy at this stage of the proceedings & so you will have to excuse me if this letter does not say very much. I am enjoying the trip infinitely more than I had expected. It is extremely comfortable & a quite pleasantly lazy life. The only exercise I take is swimming which I try to do at least twice a day.
>
> The first few days it was pretty rough, I was not ill though I had a bit of a headache for a day or two. Fortunately this is a very steady boat and my cabin is excellently situated. Day follows day now & one hardly notices the passage of time. I usually have a bathe before breakfast which is a vast meal of porridge, cereal, bacon & eggs, cold ham & the rest of it with endless fresh rolls, toast, unlimited marmalade & butter. It is difficult not to over eat. The greater part of the day I spend in a deck chair on the deck, I am sitting there now. It is quite pleasantly cool under the awnings. At various intervals I bathe, eat vast meals & consume iced drinks.

I did comment on how hot the nights were 'but there is an ingenious device for blowing a strong current of air into the cabin from two points which is a terrific boon & I sleep very well on a most comfortable bed.' I also commented on a fine school of dolphins I had seen 'and of course endless flying fish, I had no idea the latter flew so far.'

On 20 October, three weeks after boarding the *Capetown Castle* I was writing from Freetown harbour in West Africa. 'I am not absolutely certain that this letter will go off but I think it will, and may go through quite rapidly.' I was not able to say where we were anchored but I did comment on the thrill of being in a port again.

> I had thought the heat would be appalling but we arrived at the right time of year and really it has been very pleasant. One cannot land there but there has been plenty of life around to watch, it all looked rather attractive. Our stay has included the coolest day they had had this year. The local inhabitants cause endless amusement to the troops as you may imagine. They are quite adept at diving for pennies The biggest thrill I have had to date is seeing a place where there is no black out. I had forgotten that lights looked so attractive by night, especially by the sea. It is very pleasant sitting on the deck and just looking at the lights & the little boats moving about over the water.

We spent two days at Freetown refuelling and then set off again; life resumed its usual pattern. Not that the pattern was all that bad for us officers – the use of a large first-class indoor swimming pool, superb food and plenty of deck space to sit on. At this time ships still provided alcohol – and drinks were very cheap too – this was to alter a little later in the War. A letter I wrote just before we reached Durban commented on the amount of exercise I was taking playing deck tennis and also how I had become very friendly with another doctor on my draft, one John Gibbens, who had been to South Africa and had contacts there. After about two weeks we sailed into Table Bay, our first view of land since leaving Freetown. We did not anchor there but went close to the shore and had a marvellous view of Cape Town and Table Mountain with its tablecloth of cloud. From Cape Town we parted from the convoy and proceeded on our own up and close to the east coast of South Africa. It was wonderful to have land to look at and I remember thinking it looked rather like the south coast of Devonshire as viewed from a boat. In 1981 Anne and I travelled down that bit of South Africa on what is known as the Garden Route; it is very lovely. I wrote quite a long letter home just before reaching Durban on 5 November; I was clearly looking forward to stretching my legs on shore. This letter concluded:

> The war news does not seem to have altered much since I left home except for the flare up in Egypt. It will be pleasant to see a newspaper again soon. We still have the suave tones of the BBC announcer saying 'This is London' each evening. Their overseas news service is quite good except Saturdays when it is almost all sport. The day after we attacked in Egypt the news proper was read in 4 minutes, then we had 8 minutes in which I heard how Marlborough College, Cambridge University and St Mary's Hospital had done in the day's sport!

We docked at Durban in the evening of 5 November. All troopships arriving there were greeted by a buxom lady standing on the quay and singing songs; we were no exception. John Gibbens in addition to being a GP in London also held a paediatric appointment at one of the London teaching hospitals and had written a textbook on paediatrics. He had wealthy friends in Durban who entertained us right royally – the husband's father was Chairman of the Union Castle Line. We lunched with them at a big club just outside Durban and were then driven out into the country and had tea in a hotel high up and looking over the Valley of a Thousand Hills. It was a truly great experience to see that vista after so many days at sea; it still looked pretty good when Anne and I were driven past that same hotel some thirty-eight years later. We spent four memorable days in Durban. In addition to the letter which I had written just before and posted on arrival I was able to send an airgraph. These preceeded air letter cards; they were written on a single sheet about the size of a postcard and then photographed and the negatives sent to England where they were processed and sent on, much less heavy than letters and so sent by air. Letters only went by sea. My airgraph described my trip from Durban but the censor would not allow me to say where I actually was.

It was while we were in Durban that news came through of the defeat of Rommel's army at El Alamein and of the landing of American troops in North Africa. This was all an added boost. After our four days in Durban we sailed into the Indian Ocean and my only memory of that voyage is of the wonderful news coming over the radio of our successes in North Africa and of the Russian victory at Stalingrad, in truth the real turning point of the War although we were destined for a very different sphere of operations.

After about two weeks we reached Bombay. I was impressed by the Gateway to India which reminded me of the Marble Arch, less impressed by the stink of betel nut which pervaded the streets. I had been given my first posting while on board, to a military hospital at Kamptee near Nagpur in central India. Before catching my train I had time to send an airgraph telling of my safe arrival and posting and commenting on the splendid victories in North Africa – 'I would have loved to have heard the bells ringing.' Since the summer of 1940 all church bells had been silenced; they were only to be rung if and when invasion took place.

CHAPTER VI

Calcutta and 47th British General Hospital, 1942-43

My stay in Kamptee was brief; after only two days the colonel in charge of the hospital, an Anglo-Indian, sent for me and said I was posted in to the 47th British General Hospital in Calcutta. I wrote home on 1 December saying that as I was now in a 'defence zone'. I could not say where the 47th BGH was, although I am sure my parents guessed my whereabouts before long. I did say something about rail travel in India.

> After two long railway journeys I feel myself to be quite a hardened traveller. These journeys are as a matter of fact rather fun. An Indian first class carriage is about the size of 2 European ones knocked into one & one sleeps and lives in them. There is a lavatory, shower bath & washing facilities in an adjoining room. I met some very entertaining travelling companions including 2 very charming young Burmese subalterns. They were in talk and manners like any educated Englishman and were most interesting telling me of their experiences.

I continued my letter by saying I had acquired a bearer at Kamptee and he had accompanied me to the 47th

BGH. He had wanted to know if I was any relation of Sir Frederick Maurice who was once at Kamptee and was very pleased when I owned to a distant, very distant if truth be known, cousinship. I went on to say something about the hospital in which I was working, of which much more later, and also how I was shortly to go to Darjeeling for a day. I had only been a very few days at the 47th BGH when the colonel in charge asked me if I would mind escorting a trainload of troops who were going to Darjeeling on leave; all troop trains had to have a medical officer to accompany them. After eight weeks less four days at sea I could think of nothing I would rather do.

On 3 December I boarded the night train taking troops to Siliguri where one changes onto the famous mountain railway to Darjeeling. I did have one slight worry – no one had told me what I was to do when I got to Darjeeling and I would have to spend a night there before returning to Siliguri to board the night train back to Calcutta. Fortunately there was an Indian Army doctor on the train and I asked his advice; he told me there was a small Military Hospital at Labong which is just north of and below Darjeeling. He said a Captain Wigglesworth was in charge and he was sure he could accommodate me. I can still remember thinking Wigglesworth was a funny sort of name; I had never heard it before, but it was comforting to know I could find somewhere to stay. Little did I then know that Bob Wigglesworth's and my paths were destined to cross and recross professionally and socially for the rest of our working lives and beyond.

The train had left Calcutta in the afternoon and the next morning found me breakfasting in the station restaurant at Siliguri. I wrote to Tim from Darjeeling in the evening of the following day, I thought he would be particularly interested to hear about the trip.

It will be almost impossible not to bespatter this letter with superlatives. The railway up here is a little narrow gauge affair, a toy railway which accomplishes the 47 miles up from the plains, overcoming the most incredible gradients & taking quite 5 hours to do it. Kanchenjunga is visible from the bottom as a snow-capped peak & is then lost to view until one has almost reached the top when it reappears to dominate the entire scene.

The train ride is the greatest fun, there are actually perhaps half a dozen trains since one engine can only pull about 2 coaches. Every 8 miles or so we stop and take on water, & if one is energetic one could almost walk beside the train some of the way.

The foot hills themselves, little affairs of some 10 or 12 thousand feet, are covered with jungle & I think very lovely, a marvellous change from the plain which one sees far below as you climb higher and higher. But it is at the top of the line, Ghoom, since the line runs down the last part of the way to Darjeeling, that has to be seen to be believed.

It was late afternoon by the time the train reached Darjeeling and the usual mist expected at that time of year had descended; as I wrote to Tim I explored around a bit and duly contacted Bob Wigglesworth at

Labong. He had been at Barts but as usual we had many mutual friends including Hugh Blenkin, a one-time study companion of mine at Marlborough. Bob was most welcoming – he had married just before being sent out to India some months previously and I think liked having someone to talk to. I woke next morning to glorious sunny weather and can still remember the thrill of seeing the Kanchenjunga range spread out before me from Bob's bungalow, a truly unforgettable sight.

My letter continued by saying I had made the excuse of staying another day in order to collect some notes on a patient.

That involved getting a pony and riding up about 1500 feet. There are superb views all the way, with Kanchenjunga as ever dominating everything. It is at its best in the morning since there are practically no clouds and I took a series of photographs. In the afternoon I did another long walk and in the evening my host & myself again went up to the place I had been to in the morning to dine with another RAMC officer and his wife. This time we went by car, 20 miles instead of 4. My only regret is Everest has remained bashfully hidden by cloud, it is only visible from the place 1500 feet above here. There are other things I might tell you about, the delight of a hot fresh water bath, the first since Leeds as hot water is unnecessary in the plain, & of snuggling down in bed with lots of blankets & of sitting over a blazing fire. It was a superb piece of good fortune that I had to come up here, & in my first 10 days in the country too.

My journey back to Calcutta starting with the mountain railway was uneventful and I got down to work in the 47th British General Hospital. I was in the medical wing which was situated some way from the surgical wing but was of necessity much larger. Disease took a far greater toll than battle casualties in the Far Eastern war. We were accommodated in what had been a convent, various buildings scattered about in pleasant grounds containing a small lake surrounded by flowers. It was the cool season too and the climate was marvellous, quite cool at night. As I wrote home I had started the War in a lunatic asylum (Park Prewett) – at a later date spent six months in a workhouse (Amersham) – and had now achieved the height of respectability in a convent. I had returned from Darjeeling on 5 December and as I noted in a letter home on 6 December it was ten weeks since I had spoken on the phone from Leeds just before leaving for Liverpool and that was the last time I had had any news from home. In this same letter I also said how used I had become to sleeping in railway trains, four nights out of the last ten and no two nights consecutive.

I found myself working on a 120-bed ward; initially there were other doctors with me but this was not for long – they were posted on and more and more work descended on me – more of this later. My birthday was on 15 December but I celebrated the occasion on the 14th when John Gibbens, who had been responsible for my entertainment in Durban, suddenly turned up to see me. Apparently he had been posted to Delhi –

he ranked as a medical specialist – but as they had no work for him there he went to stay with Sir Maurice Gwyn, the Chief Justice of India, who was an old friend of his. He now did have a posting – to Shillong in Assam – and had stopped off in Calcutta on his way. He had no idea where I was in all India but dining in his hotel the previous night he had met a man who knew me and had told him how to find me. Not bad since I had only arrived there myself two weeks before. He told me if ever I found myself in Delhi I must get in touch with Sir Maurice – he had mentioned me to him and apparently Lady Gwyn was a relative of my Aunt Olive and he knew the family.

It was on 16 December, the day after my birthday, I received a cable from home. Unfortunately it was largely illegible but the beginning and end was 'very pleased' and 'all well here'. Anyway, communication was re-established. It was at about this time that I went to a reception at Government House and was presented to the Vicereine – Lady Linlithgow. I hope I made a suitable bow.

When I started work at the 47th BGH I had been starved of doing much doctoring apart from some at Devonport for the better part of a year and I was thrilled at being able to resume my chosen profession although I expected to be posted on before long. I thought my brother Tim would be interested to hear about my work and wrote to him on 21 December, very excited as I had just received two airgraphs, one from him and one from my mother, my first home news apart from the cable for twelve weeks. In my letter I refer to 'good' cases, a medical euphemism for interesting – much later in the War I was to become a good case myself.

> My work here is most interesting. I have two large wards, about 120 beds, and I am surprisingly free from interference from above. Malaria of course accounts for quite half the beds but in a hospital such as this (pause to kill a mosquito) there is a great variety. I consider myself pretty good at distinguishing between typhoid and typhus now! I have plenty of cases of amoebic hepatitis & amoebic abscess, some good nervous cases, pulmonary tuberculosis, gastrics, dengues (not many – out of season), some quite good heart cases & altogether a pretty good variety; and of course I get the ordinary pneumonias & so on too. Could I but stay here for a couple of months only I should really get some awfully good experience in tropical medicine as well as brushing up on the ordinary stuff. Equipment of course is not first class but X-rays are easily got & the lab is good and efficient.

For someone as keen as myself I was very lucky to have the wards on which I was working; the majority of the wards were set aside solely for treating malaria which was rampant in the Arakan and there was one isolation block for the treatment of smallpox – the more unusual or severely ill patients were admitted to my wards. The officer in charge of the whole medical wing was Lieutenant Colonel Seward, in civilian life a consultant physician at the Royal Devon & Exeter Hospital.

On 22 December I again was sent on the leave train to Darjeeling. I spent the night of 23 December with Bob Wigglesworth – it was very cold and a real Christmasy atmosphere prevailed. I was pressed to stay over Christmas but the knowledge of the workload awaiting me in Calcutta and my conscience got the better of me and I returned on the 24th, arriving back at the hospital on Christmas morning. At least I could write home on the 27th and say that I had seen snow on Christmas Eve, more I suspected than they had. As I wrote in this letter Christmas in the 47th BGH was celebrated much as in any other hospital. Last year at Amersham it had been sixpences – this year it was 4 anna pieces – in the Christmas pudding.

> Talking of Amersham it seems simply unbelievable that I still had a month to run there this time last year. I don't think, in fact I know, that I have never experienced a year which has seemed so long as 1942. Beginning with a month at Amersham I have had Aldershot, Mytchett, Bridestowe, Devonport, Plymton, Fleet, London, Leeds, the high seas and India, and with it all I have been more in Marlborough than in any year since I left Cambridge!

In this letter I wrote too how we had the usual dinner in the evening with turkey and plum pudding. I also wrote how I had been browsing in a bookshop, a favourite occupation when not working, and was delighted to pick up a book containing a picture of Lloran House in the foreground – the book, *And so to*

74

Bath, I had never read although I did know there was a copy in Lloran House.

My workload in the hospital was becoming increasingly heavy and I had little time for other activities although I did join the Saturday Club which had an excellent swimming pool and a superb library. It was in early January 1943 that I had a letter from Alice Kempson, G's elder sister, who had been doing missionary work in India, to say she was going to stay with friends, the Milfords, in Calcutta. I was able to dine with the Milfords to meet her on 9 January and the following day, a Sunday, Alice and I dined with Charles Crawford and his wife, Joan. Charles was an old friend of G's; although very senior to me at Marlborough I had got to know him quite well through G and he was now working for ICI in Calcutta. His father-in-law, Judge Roxburgh, also lived in Calcutta; it was good to have a little social life outside the Army.

On 12 January I made what was to be my last official trip to Darjeeling. By this time I was quite well known and I wrote home dwelling on the red carpet treatment I had from station officials up and down the line. Few trains had restaurant cars in those days in India – travellers fed at station restaurants en route. However I now found that while everyone else was hustled back onto the train I was allowed to finish my meal in peace before being bowed onto the train which was only then allowed to leave.

Darjeeling was looking particularly lovely – the snow much lower down the slopes of Kanchenjunga – and I stayed as usual with Robert Wigglesworth. I wished I could have stayed more than one night. Back in Calcutta it was beginning to dawn on me that I was likely to stay at the 47th BGH at least for some considerable time. The work in my ward was quite fascinating – it was a new and exciting experience to find myself treating amoebic abscesses of the liver, kala-azar and cutaneous diphtheria, a whole range of illnesses I had never seen before. On 7 February I wrote home how during the preceeding week my ward had been invaded by generals, colonels and various distinguished doctors; one such was Dr Napier, one of the greatest living experts on tropical diseases.

It was on 16 February I received a cable announcing the birth of Tim's first son, Nicholas. I wrote to congratulate him the following day. I thought I might be a bit premature but I hoped that he would take up medicine. My letter continued:

Life here becomes if anything more interesting every day. I never had such interesting and varied cases to look after at Mary's as I have here now, and I don't think I have ever had such opportunities for learning. My particular work too brings me into contact with such local people like Dr Napier, I had a meeting with him at the School of Tropical Medicine today, and it is immensely interesting to pick their brains . . . In the fullness of time I shall probably find myself in a Field Ambulance again or with a unit, but in the meantime the months spent here are just invaluable. I would just love to have Hope Cosse to see some of my chest patients!

In a later letter to Tim I wrote something about the other doctors with whom I was working. Colonel Seward, in charge of the whole medical wing, I have already mentioned.

There is far more medicine than surgery out here and the physicians live in quite a separate establishment from the surgeons. The population of this mess varies enormously in size and in the people who compose it, but there is a small, really very small, nucleus of permanent people of whom I suppose I am now one. These permanent people are I think, and I need hardly say I except myself, quite outstandingly good, both in the quantity and in the quality of the work they do. They are admirable people to work with in every way and I do think the patients get quite first class attention from them. Need I say there are no regulars among them.

In addition there are the two specialist physicians – that is men with higher degrees although actually some of the ordinary permanent nucleus have these too. One of the specialists was registrar at Kings College Hospital, the other is the charming and eccentric Duffy, part Irish and part Australian. Duffy is actually a first class physician and an admirable teacher. He fought in the ranks in the last war and since qualifying in Australia and taking his membership in England seems to have gained his experience from the whole world. He is not always easy to get hold of, though he may sometimes be found sitting in some crowded restaurant with a text book of medicine propped up in front of him, but when you do ask him to see a case he has probably seen something like it in Buenos Ayres or Sarawak or somewhere and gives a correct diagnosis.

In March things were slacking off a bit as we had a temporary increase of staff and I was sent on a course on gas warfare. This was held on the other side of India, only 100 miles from Bombay, at Deolali. Deolali is 2,000 feet high and although hot and arid it was something of a relief to get away from the humidity of Calcutta for a time. The course was boring but I was cheered on entering the officers' mess where the first things that caught my eye were four framed drawings of white horses – Cherhill, Alton, Westbury and Broad Hinton, very nostalgic. Two days before I left Deolali I received a letter from home telling me that Jim Williamson, whose parents I had visited at Bromley during the Blitz, was somewhere in the Deolali area. I managed to contact him and we had a great meeting. He was particularly pleased as he had lived in what was then Rhodesia for some years and I had seen his family much more recently than he had. We were also able to talk about his brother Dick who had been so tragically killed and whom I had seen when I visited his parents. I was able too to tell him about his brother Ken's wife, Joan, whom he had never met. We could not quite work out when we had last met – probably on the famous occasion when as a small boy our two families had gone to the Pewsey Vale to see the Cornish Riviera express go by. It never came as it had been derailed further up the line! Jim had not heard from his parents since coming to India and was delighted to hear from me that they knew his address.

Back in Calcutta I was again immersed in my work and had little time for any other activities apart from an occasional swim at the Saturday Club. However I counted myself very lucky to be gaining the experience. It was on 14 April I found myself demonstrating a case in front of forty or fifty doctors including a major general in the officers' block. As I was leaving I was accosted by Freddy Taylor – son of the one-time partner of my father, and younger brother of my great childhood friend, Peter. He was a patient in the BGH with a gunshot wound to his elbow – it was good to see him and find him looking well.

I have not said anything about the appalling conditions so many of the native population of Calcutta were experiencing at this time. The crops had failed and there was widespread famine. Smallpox and cholera were rife. It was quite possible to consume a six-course meal at Firpos – the principal restaurant in Calcutta – and trip over someone dying of starvation on the pavement outside. I still vividly remember visiting a native hospital where smallpox and cholera were being treated. Semi-conscious victims of cholera were brought in and given intravenous transfusions of salt and boiled water; this was poured in to relieve their dehydration and then they would experience a monumental rigor, but it did seem to help. I was not concerned with the treatment of smallpox but frequently found myself in contact with someone suffering from that all too frequent fatal disease. After every such contact I would vaccinate myself on the forearm; at times this was a weekly affair.

On 10 May I had a little break from my hospital work and I was sent on a Dutch hospital ship to pick up a number of sick and wounded officers and men from Chittagong. I was still really unconcerned about the war against the Japanese. I was far from the front and by the time I arrived in India Burma had fallen to the Japanese and the battle in Arakan – on the north-western coast of Burma – was virtually over. The Japs were preparing for the invasion of India which was to take place in 1944. An army corps was stationed on the India-Burma border in the Bay of Bengal to prevent the Japanese advancing any further and sickness, particularly malaria, was taking a heavy toll of our troops. I enjoyed my little sea trip very much; it lasted for five days. The boat was comfortable although my cabin was hot. The trip down the Hoogly river from Calcutta was fun and then the fresh sea breeze invigorating. The Dutch officers were most friendly and I spent a lot of time on the bridge; there was not much on the short sea trip I could do for my patients.

The hot season was now very much upon us and the workload heavy but still fascinating, although sometimes tragic. One such case that came my way was a young soldier who had been bitten by a viper while crossing a bridge in Calcutta. By the time he was admitted he was blind, vomiting blood and swollen all over, but still fully conscious. Mercifully he died within a few hours; I have never forgotten him.

Despite the intense humidity and temperatures of 108°F in the shade my work in the ward was occupying virtually all my time; I usually only allowed myself a twenty-minute break for lunch. I had also been made responsible for paying the head waiter and cook with the money they needed for buying food for our mess and was responsible for supervising the menus. However the heat was so intense that I do not think any of us were particularly interested in food, and I found I had gone completely off alcohol. Most of us by this time were suffering from prickly heat – certainly I was. I did manage to get to the Saturday Club most Sundays when I could have a swim and I did enjoy their curry lunches. On 30 May I was able to write home and say we had just had a most welcome downpour of rain; the temperature seemed to drop 20° in five minutes, a great relief. In the same letter I was able to say my present appointment was now beginning to be for longer than any I had held since qualification.

On 1 July I was informed I was to go on a three-month course to Poona. The course was designed to give four weeks training about the Army and then eight weeks instruction in tropical medicine with a month as a resident in a hospital. As my commanding officer remarked, it was lunacy to send me after all the experience in tropical medicine I had gained in Calcutta. However to leave Bengal in the hot and humid season for Poona was not an unwelcome prospect. On 11 July I was writing from Poona: 'At last I know why there is such a shortage of doctors and where they all get to, Poona – doing nothing!' However there were many old friends to meet and gossip with in Poona; one such was Gordon Barclay whom I had got to know so well at Devonport.

Gordon was not the only old friend in Poona; I

found many there from Mary's days and people I had travelled out with on the *Capetown Castle*. The journey to Poona from Calcutta meant going right across India to Bombay in order to get to Poona and my letter home on 11 July after writing about all the old friends I had met continued:

> The journey was uneventful except for a glorious incident after lunch the first day. We had stopped for lunch at a station in the extreme centre of India (no restaurant car at that stage). After lunch instead of going on we just sat in the station for $^3/_4$ hour until at last the engine gave an impatient snort and moved out. We got about 300 yards down the line when we stopped again, our carriage being on a level crossing with a good view. A very smart car came up at great speed, pulled up with a jerk, and out got a Maharajah dressed in fabulous robes and carrying a scimitar. He was escorted by an Indian major and walked down the line to the last coach and got in. A minute or two later a second huge car appeared behind the first and an excited man got out bearing a small metal case (one liked to think containing jewels) and dashed after the retreating Maharajah. Then on the other side of the crossing a third car appeared and a minute bag was borne down the other side of the train to the same coach. Behind that a minute later a fourth enormous car appeared with an especially excited man who ran down the train clutching a tiny cine camera. With that we finally got under way.

I continued my letter with a description of the country in the run-up to Poona 'very like Wales with hills and deep valleys and rushing streams'. The real advantage of Poona was the climate. It did rain for the first forty-eight hours after my arrival which meant I was moved from a tent to a hut which was much more pleasant. However the coolness of Poona after experiencing Calcutta in the monsoon was a real blessing and as Gordon Barclay wrote to my mother after our meeting, my initial Calcutta pallor soon wore off and after a day or two I developed quite a healthy colour. Actually when we first met he thought I must have been recovering from a particularly vicious attack of malaria.

The whole course at Poona was quite farcical. I wrote home on 11 July stating my life was quite unbelievably idle – there was apparently a shortage of instructors.

> Poona, one cannot help feeling, is all you would expect it to be and worse. No thought of war has ever dimmed those glaring street lights or interfered with those nightly dances; I wonder what its inhabitants [and I referred of course to British] would think of England now. I have joined the Poona Club, chiefly for the excellent library it possesses, but the place sickens me somehow.

The day after writing the above I was writing again to say

> those of us who came from that direction [I was referring to Calcutta and the East] are to return there very shortly – in fact I expect to be going back to the 47th very soon, at latest by the end of the month. This enforced jaunt to Poona came just when it was most

needed, in fact I have some regrets at returning so soon, but there is no excuse for idling here when everyone is working so hard and I shall be glad to get back into harness again.

As in many of my letters I commented on the news from home, currently the invasion of Sicily.

On 25 July I was still at Poona and wrote home how I had hunted out Tony Elverson, my old pal of Green Tree Press and *Marlborough Bird* days. He, like me, had gone into medicine and was working in a hospital at Kirkee, some three miles from Poona. We had a great meeting and the next night went together to the local cinema; as we entered I heard a loud cry of 'Dick' from another old friend of Mary's days – one Peter Parry. I tend to dwell on these meetings with old friends but when you are halfway across the world with no hope of getting home in the foreseeable future the sheer pleasure of meeting up with them has to be experienced to be believed. I said as much in my letter: 'I do love meeting Mary's people out here. Actually the gallery of that cinema must have contained enough doctors to look after half Wiltshire and so it is hardly surprising I found a friend among them.'

A later paragraph in this letter reads 'I am becoming much too optimistic about the war these days, Italy out of it before October and Germany by the summer (44), it is difficult not to think such things, but out here one is more sobered by the thought it will take 3 years yet to beat the Japanese.' Well – I was too optimistic about Germany and too pessimistic about Japan.

The very next day after writing the above we heard 'the powers that be have reached the conclusion which all of us had some time ago that a large number of RAMC doctors were wasting their time in Poona and could be better employed elsewhere.' The course itself tottered to a premature conclusion and we were told we could do what we liked until the end of the week and then get back to our units as best we could. By 2 August I was back at 47th BGH having somehow secured a berth on the Bombay-Calcutta train leaving on 31 July. I went down to Bombay on the 28th and with great difficulty secured a provisional reservation. I spent that night in a hotel and had my first hot bath since February! I returned to Poona the next day and then back to Bombay with my gear. After another night in a hotel and by practically living in the reservation office next day I secured berths with three other medics for the return to Calcutta. The journey back was spent in reading *Pride and Prejudice* for the first time. I returned in time for a late lunch and then had to do a full round in my old ward catching up. In fact my letters show I was again up to my eyes in work. 'Two illusions of mine have been destroyed out here, one the necessity of alcohol and two that of a siesta after lunch, my lunch is merely a half hour's interval in the day's work.'

My return to the 47th BGH was not to be for long. On 15 August I was writing: 'I am very thrilled because I am on the move again, in the opposite direction this time.' I went on to say I was being sent to a Corps HQ to look after the staff there. 'I should think my time with the 47th will be finally over. However I ought to get a good job when I want one from a post like this – I mean inevitably I am brought into contact with the right people!' My letter shows I was slightly worried that I might not have enough work although I had been assured it was really quite a busy job. 'Anyway I could do with a slacker job than this for a time, I was up most of last night resuscitating one patient with very malignant malaria and keeping an eye on another in an iron lung.' The weather, too, in Calcutta was at its worst and I knew that Imphal, where 4 Corps was situated, had a much better climate.

On 22 August I wrote a rather belated letter to my father for his birthday on 5 September saying I had sent him a food parcel, and the most important ingredient was 2lb of marmalade! I was supposed to leave for Imphal on 20 August but for some reason there was no train that day and I had to wait a further week. At least I was less busy as my beds had been reduced to sixty-three pending my departure.

CHAPTER VII

Imphal and 4 Corps, 1943-44

Before going to 4 Corps I must confess that I had not shown all that much interest in the Burma campaign. Apart from one small area in the north-west corner Burma had been fully occupied by the Japanese prior to my arrival in India; I was just a doctor working in a busy city hospital. In 1943 our forces were operating on three fronts. The southern front was the Arakan on the east side of the Bay of Bengal. This so far had seen the bulk of the fighting but our attempt to defeat the Japanese in the jungle had not been successful and was abandoned in May with the start of the monsoon. The central front was the state of Manipur. Imphal is the capital of Manipur and it was to Imphal that so many of our defeated forces had made their way in 1942 – a way through jungle and mountains with little food and medication before the advancing Japanese who seemed so much more attuned to fighting in the jungle. The northern front was the responsibility of the Americans and the Chinese. These three fronts were separated by impenetrable mountain ranges and there was no land communication between them.

The Imphal plain is 2,600 feet high and runs north and south occupying 700 square miles. Imphal is at the northern end; the mountains to the north, west and east are never more than a dozen miles away. The range to the east separated Manipur from Burma and the Japs. The Manipur river flows sluggishly through the plain from north to south. It then flows through a valley without tracks or paths into Burma and finally winds into the Chindwin river which is itself a tributary of the Irrawaddy. All supplies to Imphal had to come by road from Dimapur situated some 170 miles to the north and over high mountain ranges. This road had been little more than a track and great efforts had been made to construct a proper road which had been completed in January 1943. In February 1943 4 Corps Headquarters moved to Imphal. When I reached Imphal in August the Corps was composed of three Divisions – 20th Div centred on Tamu on the Burma border in a mountainous area and some seventy miles SW of Imphal to which it was connected by a road of sorts; 17th Div was centred on Tiddim which was well inside Burma and due south of Imphal. The road to Tiddim was some 162 miles in length and the last two-thirds of it only a jeep track through mountains; 23rd Div was centred round Imphal and Ukhrul which lay in the mountains some forty miles NE of Imphal.

Morale, not surprisingly, was none too good among the troops, both British and Indian, particularly in the less forward positions. At home all efforts were being concentrated on the forthcoming invasion of France after our successes in North Africa; the Far East got

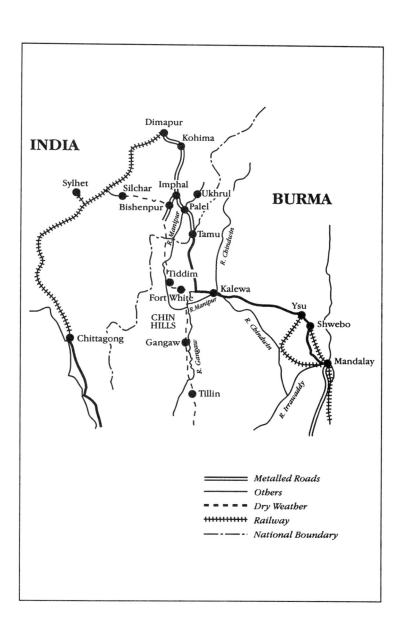

INDIA

BURMA

Dimapur
Kohima
Sylhet
Silchar   Imphal
Ukhrul
Bishenpur   Palel
R. Manipur
Tamu
R. Chindwin
Tiddim
Fort White   Kalewa
Ysu
R. Manipur   Shwebo
CHIN
HILLS   R. Chindwin
Chittagong   Gangaw   Mandalay
R. Gangaw
Tillin   R. Irrawaddy

	Metalled Roads
	Others
	Dry Weather
	Railway
	National Boundary

little space in the press or on the wireless. We had good reason to call ourselves The Forgotten Army. Wingate, with his two Brigades and supplied entirely by air, did manage to penetrate some 200 miles into Japanese territory and caused some damage to their communications. This was something of a morale booster although in fact little was achieved and 1,000 of his men – a third of his fighting force – never returned. Sickness everywhere was appalling and accounted for far more casualties than enemy action.

On Monday, 30 August, I was writing from 4 Corps HQ. Obviously, as I said in my letter, I could not describe the journey in detail; I could not say where 4 Corps was, but I did write it was a superb trip through mountain scenery at the end. In fact it involved a three-day journey, starting from Calcutta on a broad gauge railway, then changing to narrow gauge to the Bramaputra river which had to be crossed by boat. This was followed by a further train journey to Dimapur which I reached on the second night and was spent in a transit camp. The tents were pitched among a number of stone monuments, said to be fertility symbols; the troops referred to it as Penis Park. I was fortunate there as I met up with an officer with whom I had many mutual friends and he solved my transport problem which was made by truck over the long road from Dimapur up to Kohima and then on to Imphal. The scenery was truly splendid and it was great to be in mountains again after the humidity and squalor of Calcutta. One memory that sticks in my mind is the number of trucks which had fallen over the precipices (known as 'khuds') on the side of the road. The drivers were Indian and not very skilled, and the road by no means easy; fortunately we got through unscathed but arrived so late the officer who had invited me to accompany him took me to his mess for the night.

My letter continued:

> I am not sure what this job is going to be like. The man who is changing places with me has an immense reputation, I heard of him months ago, and it is never so easy following after a very good man. There are of course large numbers of troops to look after but there are also a great many very senior officers. I have been round with him today and he has been introducing me to Brigadiers and people who are his patients.

The introduction I remember best was to Brigadier Loup; he had suffered injuries when the vehicle he was travelling in had fallen over the khud; he looked at me rather doubtfully and exclaimed 'Better the devil you know than the devil you don't.' Tony Loup was the senior officer in charge of administration and quartermastering and was and is a very dear man. He retired as a major general and I have met him many times at reunions after the War, although now approaching ninety, he can no longer attend them.

HQ 4 Corps was situated close to the town of Imphal and for the most part accommodated in native reed huts, or 'bashas' as they were called. It had in fact returned to this location after a temporary and hurried evacuation due to a suspected case of plague just before my arrival. These bashas were in a wooded area with palm trees, bamboos and many banana trees, and was the site of my main surgery. However I had another surgery at the 4 Corps Signals unit and on the advice of my predecessor I slept and ate with the Signals. A Corps HQ had many senior officers and they messed separately according to rank. The Signals unit had a single mess for all the officers and the atmosphere was less rarefied. My accommodation was better there than it could have been at the HQ – 'I thought it was a cow shed but the man who lives in the next room – well, stall then – is most indignant and tells me it is a veterinary surgery. Even so I have electric light and a bed side switch, and with my camp furniture including a very nice camp armchair which I bought recently I am quite comfortable.'

One of the great pleasures when so far from home was to receive letters; by writing regularly I could expect regular replies. About every four weeks I would write to my brother Tim, particularly concerning the medical work I was doing; fortunately these letters have also been kept. The following is an extract from one written to him shortly after my arrival.

I am now beginning to find my feet in this, my new job. It is something like that of any unit MO except that there is much of it and it is so much more varied. One minute I am injecting a Brigadier with benerva & hepalon for his foot drop, and the next treating a sepoy for his guinea worm. Obviously so many of my patients are far too important to send to hospital with any trivial or in fact not so trivial complaint as is the usual practice, and so I have far more facilities for treatment than is usual. After the usual sick parades, and I have two, I plod around or go in my truck which I have in continuous use to visit various sick officers, and in addition I have some beds where I can keep people if I wish. Fortunately there is a lab and a microscope quite handy.

I think it is really all going to be quite good fun although obviously requiring a great deal of tact. I am of course doctor to my own D.D.M.S., a Brigadier, and so I can more or less get anything I need through him quite easily. What I should have felt like undertaking a job of this nature without my long experience of hospital practice out here I hardly know, but it would have been no joke. It is very interesting to see how a concern like this HQ does work. It all remains at present most mysterious to me as I wander around and break up conferences while I feel the pulses and take the temperatures of the participants.

A letter dated 5 September tells something about the conditions in which I was working.

I think my own staff as it were would amuse you if you could see it. I have two quite separate surgeries to run and spend most of my time at the one furthest from here which is where I eat and sleep. Down at the far surgery [that is at Corps HQ] I have two RAMC NCO's to run the place, they were picked out for it by the D.D.M.S. and are identical twins. I know the difference, one of them parts his hair on the opposite side to the other, but I can never remember which one I have been

93

speaking to on any particular subject. However they are a good pair and very keen. Then there are the children. Children in India in my experience are ubiquitous and a plague, being forever whining for 'backsheesh', but up here they are very different. The local population are all smiling and bright and particularly the children, and nearly every office in the place seems to keep a few tame ones to brew tea and make themselves generally useful. The twins have picked up two, Birandra and Kolachandra, aged about 8 I should think, they are a most amusing pair though conversation is not easy.

Up at this place we are somewhat bothered by monkeys, I counted six just after I had finished my sick parade the other morning and began to wonder if they wanted to come in for treatment themselves. The country round could not really be called jungle though I just long to climb some of the local hills, I hope I shall be able to one of these days. I went off to lunch at a hospital one day last week, the country really does look lovely.

An amusing thing happened this morning when I had to go to a committee meeting. After the meeting was over one of the people at it came up to me and said was I one of the Marlborough Maurices? He said he thought I must be because my voice was so characteristic. He was the Aldbourne Brown – Anthony – whom I knew to be somewhere in India because his people had told me about him when I had tea there with Tim just a year ago.

On 12 September I commented in my letter on how I had dined with Anthony Brown. 'Very nice seeing such a staunch Wiltshireman in such an extreme outpost of the Empire. It was a good meal too as he is one of the people responsible for getting the food here. There is on the whole a pretty big emphasis on bully in the mess.' All our supplies at this time came by the long mountain road from Dimapur and bully beef in tins was the simplest way of giving us any meat in our diet. In the same letter I wrote 'the best place for a meal is at the hospital where I dined last night.' This was in fact the 400-bed Indian General Hospital a few miles north of Imphal. The OC in charge of the medical division was Lieutenant Colonel Rex Tattersall and a useful contact.

My letters home at this time are not particularly interesting. I did comment that so far as I was concerned the monsoon seemed to carry no more rain than one gets in an ordinary English summer! By 3 October I wrote that the weather was getting very pleasant – maximum 75°F.

The mornings and evenings are really lovely with the most beautiful sunsets behind the hills... Flowers are nice too, and the patch of wilderness round one of my surgeries produces the most lovely sweet smelling roses, as well as the biggest bunch of bananas I have ever seen... The rats make such a noise I can sometimes hardly hear myself speak on the phone, which incidentally has now come back into my life with a vengeance.

In this letter I also comment on how grateful I am to Anthony Brown for supplying me with Horlicks.

In the course of a letter to Tim dated 14 October I wrote:

> I am learning of D's and Uncle Godfrey's advice here about sticking up to senior officers. I was asked to report some time ago about a river as a possible source of drinking water which they were anxious to use. After going into some details about what happened to the river just above the water point I said as a last resort it could by chemical means be made fit for drinking just like any other public sewer. I gather there was a good deal of unseemly mirth when this was read out at a conference of brass hats.

On 24 October I was writing:

> The work here seems to increase as it goes on, not with actual sickness as with other affairs. The G.O.C. Lieutenant General Geoffry Scoones [of whom more later] likes me to call on him from time to time to hear how all his key men are doing with regard to their health – the great line he trots out is 'now supposing you were Corps Commander, what would you do with such and such an officer?' Some responsibility if it is a Brigadier or Colonel in question.

I continued this letter by writing an officer in my own mess had developed poliomyelitis. 'I realised what was up and got him straight into hospital but he died the next day. The first case they have had anywhere round here though oddly my fifth since coming to India, it is not a common disease out here.' I then described a visit I had made to the local cinema in Imphal. 'The films shown here are usually post the last (1914-18) war which is about the best that can be said for them. The news films are a bit funny too.' I remember that visit well. The 'news film' was far from funny – it was really a trailer entitled 'Impregnable Singapore – Bastion of the East'. It showed views of Singapore with a few planes flying over it and ships in the harbour – and all this nearly two years after the Japanese had taken it. The following morning I marched into Brigadier Loup's office and told him about it in no uncertain terms. Indeed we were The Forgotten Army, low on everything while preparations were being made at home for the invasion of Europe.

However it was during this first two months of my stay in Imphal that important decisions were being made in London, Delhi and Barrackpore (the headquarters of East India Command, a few miles north of Calcutta). A new Command – South East Asia Command (SEAC) – was formed and Admiral Lord Louis Mountbatten appointed Supreme Commander over the allied land, sea and air forces. At the same time General Slim, who was a Corps Commander and had been in the retreat through Burma, was appointed to take command of the newly formed 14th Army. These two factors were destined at last to put us on the map and did much to improve morale. Mountbatten had the ear of Churchill, and Slim will go down in the history books as the greatest general to come out of the 1939-45 war, surpassing even Montgomery, and it must be said he was a much nicer man.

For my part I was determined to be recognized as a doctor, not an army officer. I never drew a revolver, unlike most doctors in the area; I should probably only have lost it anyway. As I wrote in one of my letters 'it would probably amuse you to see me ambling around with my stethoscope which I use as a kind of passport.' From time to time I might meet with a somewhat unexpected illness, and I wrote about one such in the course of a letter to Tim in November.

> I do not often get cases much out of the ordinary here but I did one this week. The D.D.M.S. rang up late one night and asked my orderly to ask me to see a Brigadier early next morning, he was passing through and staying the night in the D.D.M.S.'s mess. I went round the next day and found the said Brigadier complaining of what he called an attack of influenza and of a strained foot which he thought he must have injured without knowing it. I looked at it and it dawned on me that I was seeing a manifestation of a disease I have practically never seen, acute gout, and sure enough when I asked him he said his father and grandmother had suffered from gout. Fortunately I managed to unearth some colchicum and he responded like a charm. The D.D.M.S. was frightfully amused about it – funny how little sympathy that most painful disease excites – all the same I thought it was the prerogative of the regular army officer retd and was a bit staggered at meeting it in the field.

During November the weather in Imphal became ideal – lovely sunny days and cool nights – we even had a fire in the mess. 'I had a glorious run out yesterday to visit a place high up in the mountains. I climbed up a bit with a friend after lunch to get a most stupendous view, mountainous scenery but one could see a hundred miles in many directions.'

On 12 December I wrote:

I am arranging to take a little leave early in January, 10 days in Darjeeling, probably I shall be away about 18 days all told. I hope Darjeeling will not be too misty, the end of November is really the ideal time for it but I wanted to get settled here first. Anyway I fully intend and expect to enjoy myself thoroughly. The D.D.M.S. asked me today what on earth I wanted to go on leave for and so I explained that I frequently had to force officers to take leave and I could hardly exert my authority unless I set an example myself! The D.D.M.S. is a Brigadier and hails from South Ireland like so many of the higher ranks in the army medical service. Whereas however in most cases the higher the rank the less I like them [I was only referring to the medical service] I take a very good view of this one indeed. He is extremely good to me and always most helpful with senior officers and incidentally has a very sound knowledge of medicine. He asked me this morning who should do my job in my absence. I said I had no special views, he suggested someone I did not know and told his D.A.D.M.S. to try to get him and said whoever came 'it must be a doctor and not a medical officer.' Personally I get on very well with the General, it tickles me a lot to wander into his office and talk to him not as one of his officers but as a civilian adviser. No doubt I shall get slung out on my ear one day.

This seems an appropriate moment to say something of Lieutenant General Scoones. He had been a young officer with the Gurkhas in the First World War and gained a Military Cross and then the Distinguished Service Order while personal liaison officer to General Claud Jacob during the Somme battles. He had gained a wealth of experience in various appointments but 4 Corps was his first operational command. As Brigadier – later to be General Sir – Geoffrey Evans writes in his book on Imphal 'his expression was stern, his manner often abrupt, but those who served close to him found that beneath this severe facade he had an engaging smile, a keen sense of the ridiculous and a very real concern for the welfare of the regimental officer and soldier alike.' General Evans was his Brigadier General Staff for the first few months of my stay in Imphal. Undoubtedly many of his staff did hold him in considerable awe but I got to like him greatly and soon found he was always prepared to listen. I believe he may have found it relaxing to chat to someone who never pretended to be anything other than just a doctor and was not concerned with planning a battle. In the course of my life I have known many very senior officers in the services but Geoffry Scoones is the only one I have known while he was having to take the momentous decisions that go with the job. I remember forming the opinion that it must be a very lonely job and intensely demanding; Scoones was the right man for what was to come. I did once try to persuade him to relax a little – 'read a good novel' – I do not think he ever did!

On 19 December I wrote home to thank my mother for her birthday present which had actually reached me that day. My letter continued:

Saturday night is always kept for celebrations here and so the official day for my birthday was yesterday when the D.D.M.S. was asked to dinner in honour of the occasion. He was remarking on the comfort in which we live here in the Signals compared to Corps messes and I said I understood even toilet paper was unobtainable in Corps. He said that he had had none of that useful article for weeks and the padre at once offered to sell him a roll out of the men's canteen. The deal was promptly carried through; this is the first time I have caused a parson to sell a toilet roll to a Brigadier while waiting to go in to dinner!

On Boxing Day I wrote at some length thanking for various parcels I had received and continued:

I seem to have written a lot without yet touching on Christmas festivities ... we had an excellent duck last night which I personally prefer to turkey ... Christmas has actually been quite busy for me, but still as my excellent driver said to me yesterday, it is really better to be busy on these occasions because if you have nothing to do on Christmas day when so far from home one is apt to become a little homesick. It is not much good being that at present, home in two years is an optimistic view I think.

In fact I made it with a month or two to spare.

On 2 January I was writing home:

This has been quite a gay week with festivities both the last two nights, in fact I saw the New Year in in style. A huge party at Corps, I have never seen so many brass hats. Last night I dined there in the colonels mess, the other guests being lady nurses, two brigadiers and a major! I am off on my leave on Wednesday, it will probably take me the best part of 3 days if not more to get through to Darjeeling though I have a car to take me to the railhead [Dimapur] which is a good beginning. I am looking forward to doing that journey again though travelling is no rest cure out here.

On 9 January I was writing from the Windamere Hotel in Darjeeling describing the journey.

I left last Wednesday and accomplished the first 6½ hours of the journey in a powerful staff car, lunching on the way in a lovely and mountainous spot, meals have been few and far apart this trip as you will hear. That evening I did get a meal, quite a good one, before taking a train which deposited me at a station on the afternoon of Thursday (Jan. 6). It was a slow and leisurely journey, breakfast and lunch consisted of bully beef and biscuits though I got a fried egg and some liver at a station in the afternoon. Thursday evening found me boarding a river steamer [this was at Jorhat on the Brahmaputra], unfortunately a thick fog descended and we dropped anchor for 10 hours that night. I had quite a comfortable cabin but meals on board meant tins of bully, biscuits and hard boiled eggs, I had not so much as a knife or plate which meant

102

eating was difficult. I woke on Friday to a view of dimly discernible mountains through the fog as seen from my cabin window, however the 'mountains' dissolved into low mud flats with the coming of the sun and by 10 a.m. we were off. All Friday we chugged happily down stream, it was a glorious day, perfect English summer weather, and some of the country was very pretty with hills and mountains in the distance. After 36 hours of bully and biscuits we finally landed early Saturday morning and were greeted by a most indifferent breakfast. Being wise by this time I made a sandwich from bread and butter on the breakfast table, just as well as my next meal came at 8 p.m. that evening and it was all I had to keep me from starving. The whole of Saturday I spent in a train, very slow but not too unpleasant, it is so much better travelling this time of year in the cool weather. Last night I fetched up at a junction [Parbatipur] and after a much needed meal went to sleep on the waiting room floor until I caught the Darjeeling mail at 4 a.m. which deposited me at the foot of the Himalayas for breakfast. This time I avoided the mountain railway and took a car the 50 miles up to here, a glorious drive.

My letter continued

I went to the hospital to find Robert Wigglesworth with whom I had planned to stay had had to go on a course to Poona about a week ago, unexpectedly as these things always are. However I knew of this very excellent most comfortable hotel and they had a room for me with bath and all, it really is an extremely nice place, most comfortable and not too large and noisy.

I also wrote to Tim expatiating on the comfortable life I was leading in Darjeeling and on the food – 'after 4 months of bully beef in varying forms it really is marvellous.' My letter went on about the excellent service provided and how my initial disappointment at missing Robert Wigglesworth had been overcome. He would have been working all day and I did not lack for company in the hotel.

> A lady rushed up to me today in a great state, she knew all about me and told me Robert had sent a frantic wire to tell me he was going which perhaps fortunately never reached me. I think Robert was a great success up here, he looked after all the English families and they seem to miss him a lot.
>
> Do you remember my somewhat ruefully remarking as I changed out of my civilian clothes in September 1942 for the last time that it would probably be many years before next I wore anything of the sort? Well I have now armed myself with a very handsome sports jacket and grey corduroy trousers and feel really human again. You have no idea how pleasant it feels to wear such clothes again after so long – to have a hot bath twice a day (my first since Bombay last June) – to eat superbly cooked food – in fact to live like a Lord (& to have a bank balance of over £300!).

On 16 January I was writing home:

This has been a most marvellous week, I do not think that I could have enjoyed it more than I have except in England. The weather has been extremely good with

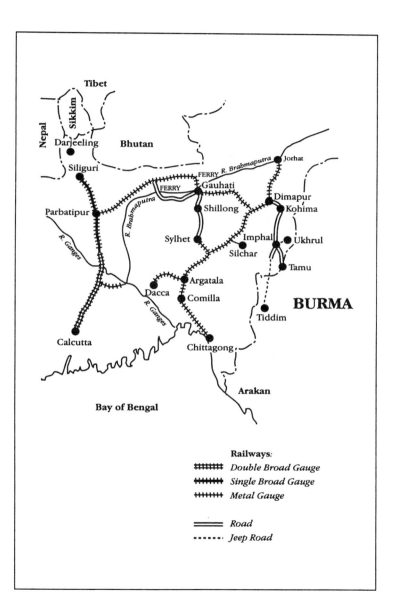

Tibet

Nepal

Sikkim

Bhutan

Darjeeling

Siliguri

R. *Brahmaputra*

FERRY

Jorhat

FERRY

Gauhati

Parbatipur

R. *Brahmaputra*

Shillong

Dimapur

Kohima

R. *Ganges*

Sylhet

Imphal

Ukhrul

Silchar

Tamu

Argatala

Dacca

Comilla

R. *Ganges*

Tiddim

BURMA

Calcutta

Chittagong

Arakan

Bay of Bengal

Railways:
Double Broad Gauge
Single Broad Gauge
Metal Gauge

Road
Jeep Road

gloriously clear days giving magnificent views of the Kanchenjunga range. The type of weather we are having is very like English winter weather without rain – frosts every night though it gets fairly warm during the day in the sun, up to about 50°F. The air though is crystal clear, rather like Switzerland.

This very nice hotel has a most pleasant atmosphere about it and it makes a very good party the whole time, there being sufficiently few people in it for everybody to know everybody else very well. I have done nothing desperately energetic, but a good deal of walking one way and another and two or three long rides on the fairly rough mountain ponies. Not much skill required there except to get the beasts to move at all. Everything is on the side of a mountain here, nothing flat at all, but there are innumerable paths to take all having the most stupendous views. One day we rode to a place about 2000 feet above here. The general fashion in the evening is to go either to the cinema or to the big roller skating rink at the club. I have not been on roller skates since I left the Malthouse but there is not much difference from ice skates and I find it quite good fun. . . The only bad day we have had except for today which is inclined to be foggy was Thursday, however that had advantages as it brought the snows much further down the mountains, in fact it snowed for a time only a thousand feet above Darjeeling. I attended a childrens party in the afternoon – something of a change from the jungle!'

My letter continued with how I had sent a pound of tea to various cousins, aunts and uncles; tea was a precious commodity in England during the War. Only one food parcel a month could be sent to any one person; my mother and Tim had already had their allotment.

On Sunday, 23 January I was again writing from 4 Corps HQ and saying my last three days in Darjeeling had been as good as any of the others. I do carry one particular memory of that stay in Darjeeling which I do not mention in any of my letters. I was doing one of my favourite occupations, browsing in a bookshop, and happened to pick up an anthology of verse. I happened to read one particular poem concerning travel to distant places and was greatly moved by one verse, the words of which I carry in my head to this day:

> But I was born in Marlborough
> And love the homely faces there
> And for all other lands beside
> 'Tis little love I have to spare.

I thought this was written by Winthrop Young, the climber, but when I asked his widow about it many years later she assured me Edward Hilton Young, later Lord Kennet, had written the poem. Sadly this was some time after I had written Lord Kennet's death certificate. I would have liked to have told him about it. Actually neither of the brothers were born in Marlborough.

My letter of 23 January was largely taken up with comments on the magnificent post I had received on my return from Darjeeling. This included my diagnostic set which I had long been awaiting and also the DDMS had managed to get me a microscope for my personal use, a great help in diagnosing malaria. I did say my journey back had been much easier than my journey out. I had arranged to get back direct without any long river passage. I had spent the night at Dimapur and according to my letter had been given two full-dress dinners and provided with a special truck for the long mountain journey back through Kohima to Imphal which I reached in time for tea. I also said that during the coming week I had to examine all ranks above that of Lieutenant Colonel to see if they were fit to go on serving. 'It was not really bad starting work again. I kicked off by an hour with the general, when I was even ruder than usual!' General Scoones came into my surgery basha and said he had come in for his annual examination. My response was 'Yes sir, certainly sir, strip sir.' This puts a young doctor at some advantage. I examined his heart and his lungs, felt his abdomen and so on. In the course of my examination I tested his knee reflexes.

'Why are you doing that, Maurice?'

'Testing you for syphilis, sir.'

They are absent in tabes dorsalis, the final stage of syphilis. The general grunted but I thought I detected a sparkle in his eye.

Years later at a reunion in London I reminded him of this incident. 'Ah,' he said, 'but what you didn't know was that I had told Brigadier Dymond [the DDMS] the previous day that I was about to go for my annual examination. "Ooh," he said, "I hope your knee jerks are all right." ' General Scoones did have a sense of humour.

108

When I returned to Imphal in January 1944 the Corps was still spread out over huge distances to Tiddim, Tamu and Ukhrul and our only source of supply by land was through the mountainous road from Dimapur some 170 miles to the north. However under Slim's leadership 14th Army was beginning to get into its stride. Medical supplies were improving and MFTU's – Malaria Forward Treatment Units – were being formed which meant malaria could be treated in forward areas rather than being evacuated over long distances back to base hospitals. Also aircraft were becoming much more available and air evacuation of the more seriously sick and wounded was beginning to become routine.

It had been planned that 4 Corps would mount an advance into Burma from Tamu and Tiddim but evidence from forward areas showed that the Japanese troops were being greatly increased and were preparing to advance on Imphal. General Slim and General Scoones had both reached the same conclusion: the right strategy was to withdraw the 4 Corps divisions from Tiddim and Tamu to the Imphal plain. This would concentrate our forces, give the Japanese greatly extended lines of supply and our troops would be fighting over open and reasonably flat ground to which they were much more attuned than the jungles and mountains. The only problem was to decide when this withdrawal should be made.

Meanwhile my letters home were not of great interest. I did comment 'The weather has turned suddenly very wet all this week' – this letter dated

30 January – 'it will freshen everything up but I shall be glad to see the sun again. It seems to have made the rats even worse, in one night they ate through my cushion, tobacco pouch and cap. I managed to catch one the next night.' I continued with comments on my social life, dining in various messes including an RAF mess some miles away. I am sure that by this time my parents were in no doubt where 4 Corps was situated although of course I could never tell them directly. In my next letter dated 6 February I wrote how I had received letters from both the Williamson brothers, Jim and Ken. Ken's ship had been sunk on his way out to India and he went to Calcutta on survivor's leave; Jim had joined him there and they had both gone up to Darjeeling, getting there the day after I had left.

This letter continued:

I am feeling slightly unsettled at the moment. I thought when I got this job it would do me nicely until the end of the war although if I wanted a change at any time I would have no difficulty in working it. Now, after only 5 months at it, the D.D.M.S. says he wants to put my name forward for promotion; sheer nonsense I think, I know nothing about soldiering at all. As a major I should have to be second in command of a Field Ambulance or Casualty Clearing Station or a D.A.D.M.S. The last named I refused point blank (he has given me a free choice of what I would like to do) and for the rest I more or less told him I was very happy as things were. However he says names don't have to go in until the end of the month, of course I shall have to let him send in mine if he wants to. I have got until then to think it over.

The trouble is I have very short service compared to most captains and know next to nothing about Indian Field Ambulances or Indian troops for that matter. Here I get on very well, it is great fun shaping 'higher policy' on a whole war front as I definitely do have a hand in from time to time – I always thought it would be great fun telling senior officers where they got off and I do that here to perfection! However I suppose the war is likely to go on sufficiently long to make it worth while taking any promotion offered, especially when it comes in the spirit it has to me. Anyway it won't come off for ages yet, and I shall probably do a course at Poona first – and so please don't spread it abroad, I may manage to convince the D.D.M.S. I am quite unfitted for promotion yet.

My letter finished with my various social engagements, two parties in RAF messes and one in an army mess. Any higher policy I refer to in this letter did not refer to how to defeat the Japanese! Nevertheless I was roped in on occasion on certain matters in Corps HQ. It must have been some time in January that General Scoones's Chief of Staff (Brigadier Geoffrey Evans) was sent off to command a Brigade – before the end of the Imphal battle he was promoted Major General and commanding a Division. His replacement arrived from somewhere in India, Delhi perhaps, and came to see me a few days later with some trivial complaint. I remember Brigadier Phee quite well, a tall gangling sort of man; I was far from impressed. A week or two

111

later General Scoones sent for me – he wanted my opinion on his chief staff officer. I said that I had seen him and thought he was in a somewhat nervous state. 'Good,' said the general, 'that settles it,' and the unfortunate man was flown out the next day.

My next letter was dated 13 February, presumably a Sunday, like a good little prep school boy I always wrote home on Sundays if I could. I did say I had hoped to make my letter especially interesting but the censor would not permit that until the following week. However I was able to say that once again I had met one of my childhood friends, Freddy Taylor, who in fact I had seen in Calcutta after his injury. He was passing through Imphal on his way to rejoin his unit and quite by chance thumbed my car down for a lift. In my letters I do dwell a great deal on these chance meetings but they did mean a lot when so far from home with no prospect of an early return and of course it meant that my parents could talk to other parents with news of their offspring.

My letter continued with news of improvements that were taking place in South East Asia Command:

and above all the appointing of its Commander. One of the best is the daily paper that now arrives by air each day and contains all the latest news and above all has nothing Indian about it. It is something on the lines of the *Evening Standard* and really is a great institution, it is nice to have a newspaper up to date again. I told the D.D.M.S. I couldn't look a gift horse in the mouth this morning, in other words I agreed to have my name forwarded for promotion; I felt I had to really but few

people can desire a crown on their shoulders less than
I do.

On 20 February I was able to write home with the
news that I had been unable to divulge the previous
week because of censorship.

The big event which occurred during the week before
the one that has just passed was the visit of the
Supreme Commander, Lord Louis Mountbatten. He
and Montgomery must undoubtedly share the honours
of being the two most 'glamorous' figures of the war –
and after all that one had heard and read about
Mountbatten I was still immensely impressed by him.
He is an amazing man; before the war a minor royalty
with a position in society and presumably a successful
naval career though I don't think I even knew he was
in the Navy; then since the war to have a hectic career
at sea with Noel Coward to base a film on him followed
by combined ops and then his present job, no man so
completely out of the common run of Indian
Commanders can ever have reached such a position.

He was here for some days and gave us the best talk
to which I have ever listened. No formal inspections for
him. The Corps officers just gathered in a room and
then he came in and we grouped round him, sitting if
a seat was available, standing if one wasn't, while he
sat on a table and talked. He is quite unbelievably good
looking; was wearing a battle dress with the rank of
admiral, general and air marshal on his shoulder, which
must have presented a problem for his tailor to fit them
all in and looked about 35, not the 41 he actually is.

His talk was amazingly witty beside compressing into

half an hour a history of what had happened so far in the war – much of it from the inner cabinet meeting side – to what was going to happen hereafter in the war. It was as he said himself a disconnected kind of talk, he would jump cheerfully from the Western to the Eastern front and back again in the same sentence, but there can seldom have been a more enthralling tale better told. Much of what he said cannot of course be passed on, but his concept of the future agrees fairly closely with the generally accepted one, Germany this year and Japan within 2 years of that, as to how it will all happen, I leave to your imagination.

After us he went on and spoke to the men, and indeed spent his time in this part of the world going around and seeing men and officers everywhere and letting them see him, which after all is half the function of a good leader. Only one thing displeased me, he looked so well, too well to become a patient of mine. After listening to him I picked up Freddy Taylor and took him back to the mess where a message awaited me to ring the D.D.M.S., the great man had done so much talking he was hoarse, had I any throat lozenges? Now this is just what I haven't; I can treat malaria, dysentery and most serious diseases, but not a sore throat. So here I was, for the first time asked to supply something for an almost royal throat, and had nothing to do it with. However I appealed to the mess – had anyone anything, and eventually obtained 1 stick of liquorice, or what the rats had left of it, and 8 throat pastilles, these unwrapped and pulled out of the padre's pocket, he having taken them from the canteen. Both these articles I sent to the D.D.M.S. with a note of apology, however I heard the next day he was expecting a K.B.E. out of them, they had been passed on and found approval!

My letter continued with how I had managed to get tickets for a RAF Gang Show which was being run by an old friend of mine, Jack Beet. The Gang Show was instituted by Ralph Reader, originally using a few professionals and lots of boy scouts. It was performed once a year for a month or more at the Scala Theatre. It now had little offshoots performing for troops in various localities worldwide.

After the show I went behind and had a long talk with Jack Beet. He was very pleased at finding me, the first old friend he had met up here, but was able to supply all sorts of news about many people he had met in West Africa, Egypt and the Middle East since leaving England a year ago, all people whom I knew.

I was a bit shaken later on to get a letter from my mother – she had shown a copy of my letter about Mountbatten to a friend of hers, Mrs Paget, who lived at East Kennet Manor. Now Mrs Paget was a friend and cousin of Edwina Mountbatten and she had passed it on to Edwina!

I can still recall that talk that Mountbatten gave most vividly. He started off by saying 'You call yourselves the forgotten army. Don't kid yourselves – you are not forgotten – no one has ever even heard of you.' Actually events did not quite work out as he foresaw. After holding the Japanese around Imphal we were to make a limited advance into north Burma and the main attack would be a seaborn invasion. However he was never to receive all the landing craft he had been promised owing to the second front in Europe and it was 14th Army with its two Corps who fought their way through to Rangoon.

As I wrote in a letter to Tim at about this time Mountbatten did tell some good stories against himself, like the one about the Indian sepoy he spoke to and said, 'Do you know who I am?' – 'Oh yes, sahib, Lord Mountain Battery.'

My letter of 27 February for the most part contains comments on news from home in the various posts I had received, but I did have something to say about an old friend of mine from Mary's days.

I wonder if you noticed the paragraph in *The Times* some months ago which was reprinted in the Mary's Gazette saying the A.O.C. Bomber Command called the attention of all ranks to the rescue of an air crew by a doctor who swam a fast flowing river and brought back each of the crew in turn. The doctor was Flt/Lt A.R.H. Mills, Sandy Mills who was a friend of mine from Mary's days and has stayed at Lloran House. He is a very fine swimmer, probably the incident was child's play to him. I had a letter from him some time ago, although a doctor he had been on several bombing raids over Germany and Italy and had spent his leave on a M.T.B. and had a lively action with E Boats, it seems a queer way of spending leave but still –.

On 5 March I was writing home about various financial matters and then continued:

I am just beginning to develop a female side to my practice, small beginnings but still – originally nurses at the hospitals were the only women up here at all but various service women, notably WAS(B)'s (Women's Auxilliary Service – Burma) pronounced wasbees have begun to arrive. Then last week the general brought his wife up here for 2 days, however she got a bit of a chest and I kept her for a week. I was on my way to visit her one evening carrying your little brown dispatch case in which I now carry my medical gear when I saw a familiar figure staggering under a load of dartboards. I just couldn't believe it was him really, I mean it is only 3 weeks since Freddy Taylor thumbed me for a lift and now to meet Michael O'Regan walking down the road seemed too ridiculous. [It was Michael and his brother John who had been sent to play in Lloran House garden when their father died in 1922, his mother still lived in the town and he had been in the same House as me in the College.] Thus although I thought it was him it was he who gave the first shout of recognition. He too like Freddy had only just come up though I gathered he had been here before. He is not living here but passing through, but he said he is likely to be about very often. He said he always gave his mother the impression he was in the middle of India and not in 14 Army as she worried so about him, however do reassure her he is not right up near the Japs and he is very fit and well.

I do remember it was rather fun having the general's wife as a patient; she had quite a bad cough but all I had to treat her with was a placebo cough mixture; fortunately she seemed to think it was doing her a lot of good. I was also able to lend her Arthur Bryant's book *English Saga* to pass the time while she was confined to the general's tent.

It was the day after I had written home on 5 March that the Japanese offensive began against the Division of the Corps at Tiddim, some 160 miles south and well into Burma. The plan had been to withdraw the 17th Division back to Imphal before the Japanese could cut them off on their long supply route; unfortunately it had been left too late. I was of course aware of what was happening but it all seemed far away and I was not unduly worried; my letter of 12 March dealt mostly about the invasion of mosquitos – non-malarious – but almost worse than the rats. One of the latter had torn up my bush shirt and made a nest out of it in the corner of my room.

It was at approximately 5 a.m. on 17 March that I was faced with the most horrendous experience of my entire war. I was awakened by a driver who said a bomb had been dropped on a unit camping close to the airstrip and beside Corps HQ which had just moved there pending the battle which was about to take place. I seized my case after hurriedly dressing and he drove me to the spot. The spectacle that met my eyes on arrival is still engraved in my mind. The bomb was what we called a daisy cutter – on landing it did not make a crater but exploded sending bits of shrapnel in all directions. It had dropped in the middle of a British anti-aircraft unit who were sleeping in their tents. It was still dark and there were bits of bodies all over the place. The injured – for the most part very severely injured – were screaming for help, often inside their fallen tents. All I could do was to go round with my syringe, and I only had one – no disposable syringes in those days – giving morphia to those crying for help. Then I dropped my syringe and could not find it in the dark. It seemed ages before more help arrived and those still living were taken away in ambulances while I stayed parcelling up the dead as morning broke. I have had to wait forty-five years to learn the exact number of dead and injured. It was written in a book I found in the Marlborough library – *Air Battle of Imphal* by Norman Franks. He writes that the bomb had dropped at 4.40 a.m. on 17 March and there were twenty dead and twelve injured. This is very much what I would have expected but several of the dead would still have been alive when I first arrived on the scene.

Meanwhile the Japanese were advancing from all sides towards Imphal. Although this had been foreseen and indeed it was intended that the Imphal plain should be the area where our forces should take on the Japanese who would have greatly extended lines of communication and supply, it had not been foreseen that the 17th Division, centred on Tiddim, would be cut off. So 23rd Division centred round Imphal had to go to their rescue and on 18 March two squadrons – one RAF and one American – began to fly in the 5th Division from Arakan, a process which took 12 days to complete but improved our morale in Imphal. At the same time the 20th Division began to withdraw from Tamu onto the Imphal plain.

All units were concentrated in what were known as 'boxes' to resist the Japanese attacks. HQ 4 Corps had moved to their box close to the airfield on about 16 March and I joined them there with the Signals a day or two later. On 19 March I began my letter 'A certain senior officer told me two weeks ago he had been too busy to write to his wife for a month. This week has been about the busiest I have ever had however I will try to get something written now . . . ' I must have been writing that letter by my tent – we were all under canvas – as I was obviously not as comfortable as usual and I was using a *Time* magazine to make a hard surface on my knee. After some comments about a calendar I had received my letter was continued the next day:

> I am writing this in a rather uncomfortable position and you will have to be content with a short letter this week, I will try to write you a better one next... The only blot on my personal horizon at present is the thought of my impending move, however I am certain now it cannot come off for a good many weeks to say the least of it. I am sorry if this letter is dull and disjointed and generally not up to standard. I am feeling very tired, it is 10-15 p.m. and a recent mug of Horlicks – that admirable beverage – is just beginning to take effect – I am going to bed.

My letter of 26 March starts with comments on news from home contained in a letter written on 14 March; the post was still getting through. Terence and Virginia Milne had been bombed out of their home. I also wrote how a RAMC captain who had heard me talking asked if my name was Maurice; like Anthony Brown he had recognized the voice although he only knew my cousin Alec with whom he had been at Marlborough College in Preshute House. The letter continued: 'I had a most charming letter from the general's wife this week (my female practice incidentally has now gone west) asking me to keep an eye on her husband as he had such great responsibilities.' I continued with favourable comments on two American ambulance drivers I had acquired: 'both big bankers in America, this is their war work ... I am afraid my letters are maddeningly devoid of the sort of news you must be wanting to know, however you need have no worries, I am very fit and well.'

The Japanese advance on Imphal was much more rapid than anyone had foreseen. The sick and wounded were being flown out as fast as possible but despite this the 41st Indian General Hospital was overflowing with patients and they too had to move from their huts north of Imphal into the box close to the airfield – all at a moment's notice – initially there were no tents available and they had to sleep in the open. I was in the fortunate position of knowing something about what was going on, not so the hospital doctors. A few weeks later after I had left Imphal I wrote something about this in the course of a letter to Tim:

Of course I was in a far better position for getting news than most people in the area. I remember one hospital

121

there, [I referred to the 41st IGH] and no one is kept more in ignorance than hospital personnel, could not make out what all the 'flap' was about and considered higher authorities were being most absurd in their demands. One evening a lot of them went out for an evening walk (one of the M.O.'s told me about this after) and on coming back went into the mess and one of them switched on the B.B.C. news. The announcer gave out that 3 columns of the enemy were advancing on the very place on which their hospital was situated, this was their first intimation. They did in fact have to evacuate eventually and the place was later burned, after I had privily removed certain fittings that I wanted for my place.

It was on the evening of 28 March our only land route – the Imphal-Kohima road – was cut by the Japanese; it was three months before it was reopened. Imphal was now under siege and the air was our only source of supply and evacuation.

Every effort was being made to improve medical facilities as my letter dated 2 April shows.

I am having a new surgery built, a superb place, almost a minor hospital. Everything is built native style and it is fascinating to watch them at work, the natives I mean because they do the building. My new quarters consist of two huts. The first has a veranda which serves as a waiting room with a broad passage leading back from that – my office on one side and dispensary on the other, and then leading into a big treatment room and a small theatre. The other building will house my staff and any patients I choose to keep in. I have always wanted a place like this and at last have got it, I think it ought really to work very well. It was sad news this week that Wingate had been killed in an air crash. I have never had any personal dealings with him myself but he seems to have been a great man.

In fact Wingate was a very strange man in many respects; he refused all inoculations against diseases and then developed typhoid, it was said because he was kept waiting for the glass of water he had ordered when dining in an hotel and so had drunk the water in the vase of flowers standing on the table.

I still have a vivid picture in my mind of that new surgery which was built close to the airstrip. The veranda could not house all the waiting patients and there were benches on the grass outside. I have one poignant memory: I saw through my office window a soldier sitting patiently on one of the benches and looking very ill. I had him brought straight in and placed on my couch – a stretcher on boxes. Hoping to have his records to hand I asked him his name – he could not speak but just stroked his chin with thumb and forefinger. His pay book taken from his pocket revealed he was Lance Corporal Beard. Five minutes later he was dead. I doubt if the cause of death was ever known. No time for post mortems then.

By 4 April there was one cause for satisfaction – the 17th Division which had been cut off on the Tiddim road met up with the 23rd Division and so there were now four Divisions less one Brigade of the 5th Division concentrated on the Imphal plain; we now had as many troops as the Japs and were on our own ground. In addition we had complete air superiority and this was our greatest card.

When I wrote my next letter headed Easter Sunday, 9 April, the Japanese were fighting on a hill only six miles away from the airstrip. The sound of gunfire was pretty constant. Nevertheless there were still film shows on a large screen in the open air – it was said we sat in the stalls with the Japanese in the gallery behind. However I was able to write 'On the whole I have been slightly less busy this last week and am steadily increasing my staff too, an Indian M.O. to help in the mornings . . . My sick bay is extremely nice with plenty of magazines and books, actually I am living more comfortably than ever before since coming abroad just at present.' I do not think this was quite true but I suppose I wanted to reassure my parents. 'In addition I am having a particularly interesting time all round as you can probably imagine; I only hope you are not all letting your imaginations run away with you – I am having a grand time which I would not miss for anything.'

The very next evening, 10 April, I found myself writing again.

I wrote to you only yesterday but as I now have a little more news am writing again today. Yesterday I said I did not imagine I could leave here for ages, probably you have the same impression at the time of writing. However I am actually off the day after tomorrow, I look forward to a new experience in travel. My new job, which I view with mixed feelings, is O.C. of an ambulance train and of course the majority that goes with it is now mine. I will send you a wire as soon as I can and as soon as I know my permanent address, I hope you will not have fits when you see the cable, I realise you may have been a bit worried recently with so much activity going on in 14 Army. Quite honestly I am sick as mud leaving this job, it has been such a grand time and particularly lately so very well worthwhile. Besides this is the last time I could want to go as I told the D.D.M.S. when he rang me up about it this evening. Things here are so very promising for a most interesting time, and I have got to know everyone of all ranks around so well and they have all been so very cooperative – well I could go on like that for ever.

Looking on the bright side I am getting a job where I am my own O.C. and that in my case is a great advantage. I do not imagine I shall travel all over India since I am staying in 14 Army, but still I shall get around quite a lot and I believe the trains are immensely comfortable and very well fitted up. No doubt Taylor will imagine it is just the job for me after my enthusiasm for trains in my youth. Still I feel a bit of a rat about it all and shall take some time to reconcile myself to the change. One other regret I have is I feel it will largely mean good-bye to doctoring, whereas here I have had quite good experience. Besides things are so organised here with my consulting room, theatre and the like except that I do not charge 10/- through the front door and 2/6 through the back it is more like a civilian show than anything else.

My letter continued with comments on a letter I had just received with news from home and also on my triumph at having correctly diagnosed a case of measles in a soldier – 'I haven't seen a case since leaving England nor heard of one.'

I was indeed sad to be leaving Imphal at such a time with the enemy only six miles away from Corps HQ. However within a very few days of my leaving they were driven off the hill overlooking us and although Imphal remained cut off until 22 June victory was really assured by the middle of May. After 16 April the Japanese were never to get so close to Corps HQ again.

CHAPTER VIII

20 Indian Ambulance Train, April–December 1944

My next letter was dated 16 April.

Well, here I am, all complete except for the majority which should be through in a day or two. It has to be ratified in Delhi or something ... It was wretched leaving the old place at such a time, I really hated saying good-bye besides feeling such an awful cad. 14 Army apparently rang up on Monday evening and demanded my presence at once to take over this show; the D.D.M.S. turned it down flat but when they said it meant a majority he agreed since he has a fixed rule about not stopping promotion. Actually he had wanted me to go to a C.C.S. (Casualty Clearing Station) as second in command, however this is what has happened. I had a very busy day on Tuesday which allowed me little time for saying good-bye, but you can imagine the number of cracks I had to face from everyone about my desertion. Everybody was most awfully nice really. I have never had so much cooperation from everyone as I had in that place which made it all the worse leaving them when I did. Everything came so easily too, I wanted 50 blankets one day and simply picked up a receiver and telephoned the appropriate brigadier; I had them the same day; it will take 3 weeks to get ½ dozen now.

On Tuesday evening I had a message saying the general wished me to go and see him. He is a strange man, most of his senior officers find him very difficult, personally I find him most charming. Quite soon after I joined the show I had a stand up argument with him over something and I have never had any trouble since. On this farewell occasion he was particularly nice and spent ½ hour telling me the whole situation, an extraordinary interesting experience, I wish I could pass it on. I must say when I joined the army 2 years ago I never thought I should have had the experience of the G.O.C. in the field discussing his plans on the eve of battle with me!

I still think it was quite incredible that he did find the time to see me that day. He was responsible for four Divisions and the enemy were only six miles away at the time and precious little between us and them. On the other hand he had made his dispositions, it was now up to the Divisional Commanders with their Brigades to do the actual fighting. The Japanese to date had proved invincible – only Wingate had shown they could be thwarted in the jungle, and he had lost a thousand men, a third of his fighting force, in the process and had not really achieved very much except to boost morale and lower that of the Japanese. However their supplies had to come from a great distance and they became under-supplied in food and arms. If the Japanese were to win the battle of Imphal they would invade India and many Indians would side with them. This was in fact the turning point of the

War in the Far East but on that day the outcome was by no means assured. All General Scoones could do was to pick up his telephone and hear how the battle was going on the various fronts; the Imphal plain was entirely surrounded. Perhaps he had to relax a little at some stage and he could do that talking to a young doctor who knew nothing about tactics in warfare.

As for the stand-up argument we had not very long after I joined 4 Corps. He had told me I could visit him in his office at any time. There was a strict rule in the HQ that solar topis must be worn and no other headgear was acceptable; meanwhile the bulk of the newly formed 14th Army were adopting the Australian type bush hats. They were much more comfortable and more becoming than the old-fashioned solar topis. We called them 'I W double-T hats' (I Was There Too Hats). There was a certain amount of aggro among junior officers that we could not wear the bush hats and so one day I decided to do something about it. I knocked on General Scoones's office door, went in, saluted, removed my solar topi and placed it on the table in front of him. The brim was frayed and the cloth on top worn away revealing an old rusty bolt. 'Sir, either the Corps order about the wearing of solar topis will have to be rescinded or I shall have to buy a new solar topi; sir, I do not intend to buy a new solar topi.' So far as I remember he did little more than give a grunt but I went on to say that his officers resented having to wear topis now that bush hats were the in thing; I then replaced mine on my head, saluted and departed. I was relieved the following morning when I studied the

Corps HQ orders for the day. They were issued each morning, pinned up on a noticeboard and signed by the Corps Commander. The final order was that solar topis need no longer be worn and bush hats were allowed.

My letter continued:

> A bit of a party on the final evening, we still were having occasional parties, and then next morning I packed, or rather my batman did, and went off to the air field. Fortunately all aerial stuff was being managed by my patients and so I got the highest priority of everyone and went off with every stick of luggage I took abroad and everything I have accumulated since. The pilot asked me where I wanted to go (it was a huge plane I had) and I directed him and away we went, the easiest bit of travelling I have ever done.

It was of course by no means a huge plane by present standards – probably only a Dakota but it might have been the slightly larger American Commando. The planes had to fly in all the food, ammunition and other requirements for an army corps of four divisions and then fly out both the sick and wounded as well as the very large number of Indian support soldiers – termed useless bodies – who were unarmed and unnecessary under all the circumstances. The planes had no seats, there were lockers under the windows which served as benches but the majority just sat on the floor. This was the first time I had ever been in an aeroplane but I enjoyed the experience – in the fullness of time it was to be my main mode of travel in the Far East.

I continued:

I stayed the night at 14 Army H.Q. and found many old friends there and took over this train the next day. This is not really my line of country, but it has been run very badly and I shall be pretty busy for some time getting it straight. It is of course most comfortable, I have a super bathroom with full length bath, bedroom, office and so on, all very nice. Two Indian doctors beside myself and some British and Indian staff. The main thing, and one which should now be seriously taken into account, is the pay. I am now a commanding officer and my pay comes to something in the nature of £1000 a year and my keep! [This was a great deal of money in those days.] I propose buying a wireless as soon as I can get hold of one, mainly for my troops who get a pretty boring time. The runs we do vary over a certain area and I expect I shall settle down and enjoy it, I expect to carry some of my old patients fairly often anyway. All the same as a job it cannot compare with the last one I had in either interest or enjoyment. Already after 3 days I have begun to learn something about railway running and spend some of the time travelling on the foot plate trying to get the thing to move a bit faster. The people who got me here are all very emphatic that it is a very important job and are most annoyed with me for saying I did not think it was half as important as the last one, still it is much better paid and even the general said I must take promotion when offered.

The map on page 89 shows the route we covered. The distance from Chittagong, which was our main base, to

Sylhet, our furthest point, is approaching 300 miles. Comilla was the HQ of 14th Army and the majority of the casualties from the Imphal battles were flown there. We took them to Dacca, which had a large hospital, to Argatala, a little way north of Comilla and was the junction for Dacca and Sylhet and which also had a hospital, and sometimes to Sylhet from whence they were taken by road to the hill station at Shillong. The more serious cases would be taken to Chittagong which had a hospital and from whence they could be evacuated by sea to Calcutta. I reckoned to travel about a thousand miles a week. However as I said in my letter of 23 April I was still feeling very homesick for Imphal although many of the patients I was carrying were able to keep me up to date with events there.

On 30 April I was writing home acknowledging various letters I had received, but the latest was dated 2 April, ten days before I left Imphal.

> Your letters inevitably do sound a bit worried about me, I realised of course that you would be, but I am ashamed to say that I have never been in any immediate danger except from the odd bomb although one used to hear an awful lot going on quite close and I was treating battle cases first hand – I only wish I was still there. Actually all is now completely O.K. there, I expect you will know that by the time you get this.

The Japanese had been driven away from Imphal itself although the battles around were still in full swing and it was still cut off by land. 'This job is wearing to say the least, the only relaxation I get is in the place where

I have a bathe if I can, we are never anywhere for more than a few hours.' The 'place' was Chittagong. Half a mile along the railway track from the station was a large lake much patronized by the troops who could get a good cooling swim there. My letter continued:

I have been so spoilt by being able to go straight to brigadiers when I want things done I have found some things here very irksome, I hate official channels. When I got here this afternoon the R.T.O. (Railway Transport Officer) came on board and said a brigadier who was responsible for all railway movements in India was waiting on the siding for me. He seemed quite awe struck himself at having so important a person – it was just the man though for me to complain to! I asked the name of the brigadier and was told it – Boucher! [The CO of the Buffs when I had been their MO in Devonshire in 1942.] He caught sight of me as we came in and nearly fell over backwards in surprise – I knew after I left he too had left the Buffs and gone to India and well – there he was. It was grand to see him again – and of course I could do some straight talking and he has asked me to report to him direct to G.H.Q., altogether a real bit of luck, I feel slightly better about the whole thing after seeing him again. He did not know I was in India and really was quite staggered at seeing me on the train as O.C.

In the course of my next letter dated 7 May I wrote:

You remember my friend Bob Wigglesworth who had left Darjeeling when I went to stay with him. Well he has just got a job on my line of running the evacuation of patients generally. There are various staff captains at different places who organise the show, a mouldy sort of job for a doctor, even worse than mine. I saw him on Friday when we picked up a load of patients and took them to another place [Argatala] where we had not previously carried a load to but are likely to fairly often in the future. On arrival there I saw the colonel who commanded the hospital we were supplying and the captain in charge of the motor ambulances which take the patients from me. After we got the whole thing going the captain said 'I suppose you have been out here 2 years now.' I was a bit shaken and said 18 months – then conversationally – 'how long have you?' He replied it was 2 years since he last saw Marlborough. 'How is your mother?' This shook me, he was wearing sun glasses and I hadn't an idea I had ever seen him before. I apologized and said you evidently know me but I am afraid I cannot place you, he looked very taken aback and said 'didn't you realise – I am Tony Hallows.'[1] Of course I realised as soon as he took his dark glasses off. We had a great chat after that (he must have thought I was very cold at first). He had only reached this part of India the previous day. I am likely to see him quite often in the future, in fact we shall have to cooperate quite often in our work, a situation which strikes me as rather humorous.

Tony's father was the full-time school doctor at Marlborough College and he and my father really never hit it off.

On 14 May I wrote saying at last things were a bit

---

[1] I next saw Tony Hallows and Bob Wigglesworth on the same day at our Golden Wedding celebrations on 15 November 1997.

slacker which meant I had more time to get things organized. First and foremost it meant improving the food. All troops fighting on the Imphal plain were on half rations; I had been myself for some time before leaving and in fact weighed well below nine stone. Only tinned meat, bully beef, was ever served on the train when I joined it and I reckoned our battle-worn patients from the Imphal plain deserved something better than that. It was only possible to get fresh food if near a depot in the mornings, seldom the case, and so I had hen coops constructed underneath the coaches and kept goats in the guard's van which meant we could have fresh food always available. I also bought a large and expensive wireless. 'It really is essential to have some touch with the outside world... It has beautiful reception from the B.B.C. and altogether makes a lot of difference both to me and even more to my British staff who have more or less appropriated it.'

Although life on the train was obviously less exciting than life with 4 Corps it was not without interest and as my letters show it was fun to improve the facilities available for the sick and wounded we were carrying – some of whom were my old patients. Sometimes I had other guests on the train too.

22 May.

> One interest I do get out of this job is the guests I carry from time to time. I take anyone covered by the Geneva Convention. Yesterday I took a Red Cross Commissioner; a most interesting man who is head of the Red Cross for the 14 Army. The day before his trip with

me he had been dropping supplies by parachute on our troops in Burma. He told me the most harrowing personal story I have heard in the war. He has been out here for 16 months. Three months ago, before he had his present job, he had to go to an important conference. He went by air, was on the airport 12 hours where the conference took place and then flew back again: and the airport – well it was somewhere in the West country. He could not communicate with anyone while there and his wife still does not know. It would have taken a mighty big guard on that airport to keep me in.

29 May.

I recently tried bribing an engine driver with curry and rice, sweets and cigarettes and we did a run that usually takes between 5 & 6 hours in 3 hours and twenty minutes. The trouble then was that no one had any warning of our arrival at the far end and no arrangements had been made for unloading us. I ran across Tony Hallows again the other day and he came to lunch on the train. . . I carried quite a number of my former patients yesterday who all said things were very boring up there and I was well out of it. [I went on to say I was seeing quite a lot of Robert Wigglesworth.]

5 June – written the day before the Normandy landings. By this time I was well pleased in the way the train was organized as the following rather long extract shows:

I have got things much better worked out now and my patients are becoming increasingly effusive in their praise. These trains are very comfortable and my job is more that of manager of an hotel than anything else, D often said he would like to run one and I just about am. The patients always used to have tinned food, it is over 3 weeks now since any tinned meat has appeared. Luckily I have very good Indian cooks to cook the British food and refinements like bread sauce with the roast chicken are easily made. The Red Cross is an enormous stand by, they give me large numbers of toilet necessities and I supply the large number of officers and men that we carry who literally have nothing at all with tooth brushes, razors, towels, pyjamas and everything else. The hospitals should really be doing all that but they don't seem to be getting them there. Sweets are another thing the Red Cross give me to dish out. I have managed to get hold of some magazines and as soon as the patients come on they are supplied with them for the journey, but I want lots more, their life is not long, can you help me there? I have a loud speaker attached to my wireless set and a point to which I can plug it in in the first ward car in which we carry British troops and officers. I usually keep this up my sleeve and then if the train stops, as it often does, round about the time a meal is being served, I get someone to plug it in and give them some light music from London. To people fresh from the Burma and Assam jungles, and those are the people we carry very largely, the whole outfit makes a big impression. One officer fresh from Burma told me it was the best organised show he had found in India yet and a colonel yesterday complained because there were no dancing girls, he said we had thought of everything else.

My staff are tickled to death by the whole thing now since so much appreciation is shown. There is a good deal of dressings to be done and some quite interesting cases but not much medicine really.

A letter dated 11 June was mainly about a social visit I had received from a brigadier who was a friend of two of my uncles, Godfrey and Jack. Apparently I did know of his existence and had heard the story of how Godfrey had nearly drowned him off the coast of North Africa. He had heard from Godfrey that I was at 4 Corps HQ and had somehow traced me to the ambulance train. It was only right at the end of quite a long letter that I mentioned the Normandy landings. I do remember when I first heard about it on my wireless when we were in Chittagong, but somehow it was all so far away and we were in a different war.

18 June.
You do not quite understand about the goat – that is the rations. Meat goes bad very quickly in this country and so it arrives alive – in the form of a goat, I have as many as four at a time. The killing is a great ceremony, much saying of prayers and slitting of throats; I am not present. For the matter of that the chickens have to have their heads chopped off with a prayer before each one – it is like a Good Friday service if we are killing about 30, again I am not present. The electrical apparatus on the train is defective at the moment and we are having the batteries charged for a week, which gives us a week's rest. The trouble is that we can have no lights or fans, and it is not much fun living on a

railway train under these conditions. The monsoon has broken with a vengeance and the rain is fairly streaming down, some of it I regret to say through the roof.

25 June.

I am finding the second front more interesting as it progresses, certainly my wireless is an immense boon these days. The Forces and Overseas programme from England is just as clear as it is on your wireless, very likely clearer by what I remember of it. It is very interesting to hear it going steadily on, it is amazing to listen to the repeated broadcasts from Normandy itself; the shelling of Cherbourg makes an appalling din on the train! The news from Italy and Russia is good too, surely Germany cannot survive a 3 front war for more than 6 months. My *Times Weekly*'s are arriving quite regularly, they say practically nothing about the Burma Assam fighting which is a bit disappointing as I now have them up to the end of April and I had hoped to see what sort of impression you were getting in England. A great thing the Manipur road being open again. Tim would love to travel over that highway, it is really fascinating from a scenic point of view.

I have been stationary all this week but am off again tomorrow. There has been quite a lot of sun in spite of the monsoon and I have bathed most days. There has been an amazing change in the tropics while I have been in India. Whereas topis were considered essential and everybody wore shirts when I first came now topis are just about out altogether, thank goodness because they are horrible things, and quite 50% of the troops do not wear shirts even at this time of year.

3 July.

Your concern over my railway travel and its dangers amuses me because you can have no idea what the railways in this district are really like. Take an ordinary passenger train such as passed me this morning. There is of course no corridor. Each coach, and they have no compartments, is jammed full of humanity, perhaps one third on seats, two thirds standing up. Then there is the roof – each coach contains about 30 on the roof where they sit quite comfortably. Less comfortable is the lot of those who stand on the steps outside holding on to the doors – about 8 to each door. Between each coach one sees about 6 people, they stand on the couplings and cling on to anything they can – not too bad except when the train brakes which diminishes the space in which they are squeezed. Most perilous of all are those who cling to the outside of the back of the guard's van. The general impression is not of a train at all, you can barely see that, but of a large quantity of humanity travelling along under some mysterious volition.

9 July.

I get quite frequent news of my old friends at 4 Corps still from patients. Sad news this week, the signals major who was in the same billet as myself during the time I was with them has been killed. Mountbatten, as you may have read in the papers, was one of the first people to drive up the Dimapur-Imphal road after it was opened; the first lorries to go up contained only beer. There is no doubt Mountbatten is worshipped by the soldiers. He told one lot that he might give them a message of congratulation, but he wasn't going to. He remembered once when after a particularly dangerous night operation he had such a message from his admiral – but he was darn sure the silly old fool had been asleep in bed while he was on the job. He told them too that the second front had obtained its first great objective – a deep water port so it was no longer necessary for the Yanks to go to Blighty first before getting to France – and that did raise a cheer. [This was a reference to the fears – not unfounded – that many Americans were having affairs with their wives while they were far from home.] I suppose the story of Eisenhower and the King is stale to you. The King saying 'you know Monty is pushing himself rather a lot these days.' 'Yes' replies Eisenhower, 'I sometimes wonder if he is after my job.' 'Oh, thank God for that, I thought he must be after mine.'

On 16 July I was writing to say that I was expecting soon to have to make a flying visit 'literally' to my old haunts. I was summoned to give evidence in some court martial case in Imphal. I do not remember the details of this, a case of desertion, I believe, and I suppose I had to give some evidence about his mental state. Anyway, as I wrote, I was delighted, particularly as it meant I could recover a walking stick I had left behind.

On 23 July I was writing from my old address of 4 Corps HQ. 'I abandoned my train at a place [Comilla] late on Thursday night and flew up here on Friday morning. It means flying through some cloud this monsoon weather but fortunately it seems to remain very clear down below.' I do remember this flight very well, I was the only passenger on the plane which otherwise contained an enormous cargo of eggs. I reckoned that if the Japs, some of whom must have been below us at times, did shoot us down we ought to make a very good meat omelette. My letter continued:

> You can imagine what pleasure it has given me to return and see my old friends again. A good many changes as always but still a very large number of good friends left. Everybody in very good heart of course after successfully beating the Jap, I am sure that people at home do not realise that this has been a major victory out here and not merely the saving of what was at one time a very grave situation. The Corps Commander soon heard I was in the area and promptly sent messages I was to go and see him which I duly did this morning. He seemed very pleased with himself, which he has every right to be, and in the course of an hour put me right up to date with everything, all very interesting. I sent you a *SEAC*, the daily newspaper, a week ago, which gave a very good account of 4 Corps' war together with a photograph of General Scoones which I thought might interest you. The general seems to think he is one of the people anyway who has contributed to Tojo's downfall.
>
> The country here is looking as lovely as ever, more so after a little monsoon rain. The view from where I write this is really lovely, trees and mountains seen through Scotch furs in the foreground, it is a fascinating part of the world; I was really thrilled when the familiar landscape took shape again as I landed. Tomorrow I have been asked to go on an expedition

up into the mountains which promises to be very good fun. The real business which has brought me up here does not take place until Tuesday afternoon and I have arranged to fly out on Wednesday. In fact the whole party has been nothing but a little leave really and lovely surroundings with plenty of friends about, and everybody in holiday mood now with the relaxing of tension.

My next letter dated 29 July had me back on the train. I started with comments on the news from home; my cousin Jack had been killed on the beaches of Normandy and was given a posthumous DSO. I then continued with a further account of my Imphal visit.

The rest of my visit went off as well as the first part. On Monday I did a long trip with two friends in a jeep. We visited recent battlefields littered with Jap rifles, helmets and hand grenades, the latter we treated with considerable respect. We went some way into the mountains actually to plant a cross on the grave of a friend who had been buried where he was killed but the track was too muddy even for a jeep after a time. However it was all very interesting and I was able to get a much better picture of the whole show. We got to places which had been fought over a day or two before. The prisoners we are taking there, and I have seen many, are miserable specimens now. One almost feels sorry for them.

According to General Evans's account of the Imphal battle many of them had been reduced to a diet of boiled grass and slugs! My letter continued:

Altogether the whole time I spent up there was extremely enjoyable. It did mean a lot seeing everyone again – I wonder how I should have liked it there all the time. I asked General Scoones if he enjoyed his job – he said 'enjoy' was not the word he would use but, although he supposed it was conceited he liked feeling he was doing a job better than anyone else could – 'but', he said, 'there were many moments when I could cheerfully have said "Maurice, you can take the beastly Corps!"'

I somehow think he used a rather stronger adjective than 'beastly' but no doubt I did not wish to shock my mother with her Victorian upbringing.

I flew back from Imphal and spent the night at 14th Army HQ at Comilla with Robert Wigglesworth. Bangladesh is notoriously low lying and subject to flooding and there were numerous ponds, or tanks as they were called, dug out round the headquarters area. Bob was annoyed the following morning because his Indian servant, or bearer as they were called, did not show up. Then we had a message to go outside to one of these tanks – there were two dead bodies in the water, one of whom was his bearer; what had happened we never knew.

Much of the letter I wrote on 6 August was taken up with comments on the war news from Europe; I called my dining room the chart room as I had lined the walls with maps of Europe to show our advances with the aid of little flags. I also said I was delighted that the letter I had sent about the value of the Red Cross was being used at home for propaganda purposes. I went on to say:

> I do not suffer from repeated inspections; it is in fact surprising how much we are left alone. However last week I had a W.A.C.(I) (Women's Auxiliary Corps (India)) lady who came about the feeding. She is a dietician who attends to all such units. As soon as I mentioned I served ice cream whenever possible she was so impressed she hardly bothered further. However we did have an enthusiastic conversation about food for the patients in the course of which she said 'you must have had a very good mother'. Being me of course I immediately disclaimed any responsibility you might have in the matter – said you couldn't boil an egg and gave all the credit to Daddy and the scouts.

I followed up this letter a week later writing:

> I had the lady who said I must have a good mother travelling on the train this week on her way to the D.D.M.S. 14 Army to make a report on the feeding on ambulance trains. Menu for dinner – soup, a very nice fish, roast duck (stuffed), green peas and new potatoes, ice cream and egg savoury. At last I am beginning to put on a little weight – as I was down to about 8 stone 6 I can do with it – I am up about 5 lbs now.

The war news from Europe with our advances in France continued to call for much comment in my letters home. On 20 August I was writing:

> The fact that I have a powerful radio seems now to be known up and down the line and wherever we are

there is always quite a crowd moving in to listen to the news. This has been an exceptionally social week anyway with people in to every meal, I have had as many as four extra to breakfast alone... We had an amusing incident two days ago when we went into a siding which had just been laid. There was a heavy storm an hour before we went in and when we were half way in the centre of the train began to heel over. The engine stopped and we rather hurriedly evacuated our patients; meanwhile the whole line very gradually began to tip up. It looked as if I might be able to go on leave at any moment, however after a few hours they got the couples jacked up and uncoupled half the train and repaired the line sufficiently to get it out.

We were much less busy now in the ambulance train service, hardly enough work for the three trains which were responsible for the movement of the sick and wounded. One of these trains was commanded by a Major Baxter who was a keen Freemason; Bob Wigglesworth, who was responsible for organizing our movements, complained that he had to organize all our journeys to coincide with his Lodge meetings! On 3 September I was writing:

Sep. 3 is a Sunday again; it does not really seem 5 years since we sat in the consulting room with David Howell and listened to Chamberlain's speech. Somehow I never expected to hear these old names Arras, Amiens, Verdun and the like being trotted out again. Twice a day I make the most sweeping advances with the pins on my map, today we are in to Belgium and by the time you get this we ought to be well into Germany and the

146

last doodlebug will presumably have had its day. . .
Nothing very exciting has happened to me this week.
We are still very idle and I arranged yesterday with the
O.C. of another train to take those of our British staff
who wished to come down to the sea for a bathe. It
was a nice day and quite cool, very pleasant on the
beach where there was a strong wind blowing. The sea
was very brown in appearance since the monsoon stirs
up all the sand but the bathe was well worth while; the
first sea bathe I have had since Durban.

Another 6 weeks now and the weather should start
to get reasonably cool although except for one bad
spell about a fortnight ago it has not been too bad this
year. Have you seen the film *San Demetrio – London*,
very good I thought it when I saw it some days ago.

Many of the letters I wrote home during those three
years overseas referred to films I had seen; when I was
on the ambulance train, they were for the most part in
the Chittagong cinema.

On 7 September I was writing to my father having
forgotten to write to him for his birthday on 5
September:

Nothing very exciting has happened to me recently and
really I am beginning to feel I have exhausted the
possibilities of this job which now runs itself in the way
I want without any impetus from me. However I am
not expecting to stay on the train very much longer, in
fact once again I have advance information of a
pending move. I have always made it quite clear to
everyone that 6 months would be about my limit and
having now had 4½ I gather that 6 months will in fact
about see me out.

As for my next job, this is still clothed in secrecy though a rumour has reached me about that too, and although it promises to be purely administrative on the whole I think it may not be too bad; as a matter of fact it was suggested to me some time ago. It is unfortunate that in the army one cannot get on and remain a doctor, but on the other hand after doing a year of army medicine in India I have exhausted most of the permutations and commutations that one is likely to meet and am prepared to settle down to earn enough money to relearn doctoring again, and I shall be retaining my rank and therefore my pay when I leave here.

In a letter dated 11 September I wrote that I did not expect to move anyway until November.

In the meantime I have had a letter from Ken suggesting a holiday with him and Jim during October; they are thinking of Darjeeling and then perhaps going into Sikkim. If I am still with this unit I shall accompany them, it sounds most promising, and although before when I had leave I sought the flesh pots of quiet comfort now I am all for a bit more enterprise. Honestly it would be quite pleasant to go back to bully after all the roast duck and ice cream I put away these days, but I still have to maintain a high standard in my 'hotel'. Some officer patients were pulling my leg last night – they said I really ought to wear tails for the evening meal. . . I am sure you would say I was looking very fit if you saw me now. I dare not boast about health in this country though, where amoebic dysentery may strike one down at any time and without warning.

I managed to get quite a lot into my next letter written on 17 September. I still remember the ride down a mountain road in an ambulance very vividly. After first saying I had received no further news from Ken Williamson and arranging leave in Darjeeling I wrote:

I have had quite an entertaining week really; my job becomes increasingly social but I am not sure whether my train's popularity among visitors is due to myself or my cook. I had a very nice fellow on board on Wednesday who used to be medical registrar at U.C.H. and with whom I had many friends in common... We spent a pleasant evening first at the club [we were in Dacca] then at a convalescent depot and finally dinner on the train. The next evening we were at another place [Sylhet] where the non-arrival of my patients who had to come a long road journey [from Shillong] kept me 24 hours. The colonel from the local hospital and someone else from it came to dinner that night and the next day I started on a long drive to meet my patients by way of passing the time. After about 40 miles I met the A.D.M.S. of those parts, I was in an ambulance, and he took me in his car up a beautiful mountain road until we were about 3,500 feet up where we had lunch before I came back in an ambulance with the patients. Over lunch the A.D.M.S. told me stories about Uncle Godfrey and Jean in Khartoum, I expect they would remember him, Fred Escritt.

It is surprising how frequently senior officers would come to me with memories of Godfrey and his nieces, my cousins Jean and Griselda. He had been PMO in

Khartoum and being a bachelor, Jean and Griselda alternately used to take long holidays in Khartoum to help in his social life before they married. Could there have been an element of nepotism in the very favourable way I was treated by the Army in the Far East? No, perish the thought!

My letter continued:

Coming back was a hair raising business, Sikh drivers are always the most villainous and I was in the leading ambulance. We shot past precipices passing the place where an ambulance had previously crashed into a gorge killing 6 people, and so finally reached the bottom. It was then, and only then, that the brakes failed. We mowed down a crowd of people who had just got off a bus and finally finished in the bank; I thought we should have killed quite a number but could only find a few broken ribs among the lot.

Since starting this letter I have been drinking a glass of beer with Jack Maurice. [He was my second cousin – grandson of Oliver Maurice who had been a well-known doctor in Reading.] I think I had forgotten his existence if I ever knew, but he heard of my being here [Chittagong] and sent a car for me to visit him, he is a lieutenant colonel. He is stationed in my principal place of call. He won a large sum of money yesterday on the St. Leger – very pleased with himself. He said he had largely lost touch with the family and seemed very pleased to meet me. I should say his activities are mainly racing and poker but he seemed to be doing quite well. Amazing to find a Maurice here, I was staggered when I learned it – told him Tim's latest has the same name as his grandfather.

150

I was to meet him again some eleven months later and completely failed to recognise him. He had some excuse for not recognising me as I was somewhat disfigured at the time.

By 24 September I was writing to say my leave was definite and I would be leaving for Darjeeling on 6 October. I did not see much hope of getting away to a new job in the near future, as there was no one to take my place, but it could easily run without me for a month.

> No great excitements this week, my body is a nice brown through repeated bathing and sun bathing and anyone who looked less as if he wanted to go on leave I have seldom seen, in fact everybody comments on how well I look. Somehow or other I still retain a good deal of energy in this appalling climate, however after a really hard leave maybe I shall look forward to a good rest on the train again.

On 2 October I was in Chittagong, three days before my leave was due to start. Things were apparently still very slack; I was shortly going down to the sea for a bathe.

> Really my leave has worked extremely well, it is going to be a bore when I get back home and have to do things for myself instead of telling other people to do them for me. Without stepping off the train I have arranged, or have had arranged for me, an air passage to Calcutta and transport to and from the air port at either end. I have wired to Jim [Williamson] to reserve

me a berth on the train and he has wired back today to
say he has one for me on the 7th, the day I asked. . .
I hope to meet one or both of the Williamsons in
Calcutta – Ken is hoping to fly there but if he cannot
get a plane will join the Darjeeling mail on the way. . .
The weather is very hot just now and I am longing to
get cool again. Some time during the second page of
this letter my transport came and I had a very pleasant
afternoon bathing and sun bathing on the sea shore.
There can seldom have been anyone less in need of a
month's holiday than me.

On 7 October I was writing from Calcutta where I
was:

. . . staying with a friend of mine who now conveniently
commands a unit in the place. Extraordinary to think it
is over a year since last I was in Calcutta, it certainly
does not seem like that. I picked up various messages
from Jim in different hotels and clubs in the Town; it
began to seem like a treasure hunt; but anyway as I
expect you know [I assume I knew Joan Williamson
was staying at Lloran House at the time] he and Ken
got here earlier than they originally expected and have
gone on to Darjeeling to prepare the way. I hope their
efforts are proving successful, I suspect the place will
be packed out there. Fortunately a friend of mine is
now commanding the convalescent home there and so
I can always stay with him if necessary and am not
really worrying.

Calcutta has been much more successful than I had
anticipated; the whole Eastern world seems to have
assembled there this week. I have run into countless

old friends all over the place quite apart from those whom I used to know when I was here, and the whole visit has been very satisfactory. There is one man whom I especially wanted to see to do a little wire pulling for my next job, only I thought he was 300 miles away. By great luck though he came here the same day as myself and has now just left for Delhi where he should be able to fix me up before going on to Kashmir for his leave. In fact this has been the best 2 days to choose for being in Calcutta for the whole year.

There are very few people that I still know at the hospital but it was pleasant to see those few and to find the old place going on much as ever. I dined last night with Bruce Stanley whom Tim will remember, he was at Mary's and is a surgeon, I had met him in Imphal before. It was good to have another long Mary's gossip. Oddly enough he was staying at a hotel and sharing a room with a colonel I know well and with whom I lunched today, but then as I say the place is full of old faces; walking down Chowringee [the principal street] is rather like walking down Marlborough High Street. Tonight I am off to Darjeeling and I should meet the Williamsons there about mid-day tomorrow, they are going to have the advantage over me of being in training now after having had 4 days to acclimatise. Incidentally I have forgotten to mention that Tony Hallows has twice lunched with me recently – I expect you know from Mrs H.

On 10 October my address was 2 Marjorie Villas, Darjeeling where Jim and Ken were staying with some people called Synge who very kindly squeezed me in too; they had a small boy and girl, the former destined for Marlborough. After commenting on the weather which was unexpectedly cloudy my letter continued:

> We are off tomorrow for 10 days and today has been pretty hectic buying food etc. We are taking a colonel and a bombardier too, a most odd mixture although they both seem quite pleasant. The colonel is R.A.M.C. and commands a hospital out here, he had a consultant practice at Tiverton in Devonshire before the war. I think the expedition promises to be a great success, it should be anyway after the hectic time we have had getting ready this last 48 hours.

Nowadays trekking in the Hymalayas has become quite a common pastime but for me in 1944 it was the thrill of a lifetime. Jim Williamson wrote a detailed account of our adventures each day, an account that I still have, and Ken wrote many letters to his wife, Joan, who was staying at Lloran House at the time. However I think it is worth reproducing my own letters describing our trek – both were written from the Planters' Club in Darjeeling where I was staying after we had completed our journey. The first was dated 21 October – amazing how much I could cram into a single air letter card.

> Ken seems to have so faithfully chronicled our journey in so many letters to Joan since we left that I feel this will be a very poor effort beside his saga. Each night he used to write something putting all the rest of us to shame. I am afraid there will be no map large scale enough for you to follow our route unless possibly G

(Kempson) has some, but roughly it took the form of a circle covering the South West corner of Sikkim & back through a bit of Bengal at the end. The first 5 days, covering most of the Sikkim part of the trip, the weather was not too good, no rain but the snowy peaks usually obscured by mist. The country itself though was lovely, not unlike the alps in summer, while the path mainly led us through forest country. The only unfortunate thing for me was that the very first day I began to get trouble with my right knee... We dropped 5000 feet that day and that was too much for it.

From Darjeeling we had descended to a river which we crossed by a rope bridge; my knee was so painful going downhill that I began to feel I could only go uphill and in front of me was Kanchenjunga which is the third highest mountain in the world and had never previously been climbed!

However after a day or two of some difficulty going down hill (it never affected me going up) I put on elastic bandage and had little further trouble. The forest bungalows were all most attractive, very comfortable and clean, and had lovely gardens round them. [Unlike trekking in Nepal where hike tents are usually the only accommodation in Sikkim and Bengal we were always able to sleep in rest houses.] On the fourth day out we reached a place called Pamionchi, which was about 6000 feet, and has a most wonderful monastery. One of the Llamas (sic) took us all round, wonderful paintings all over the wall. Jim began to question the Llama about levitation and was told the head Llama could raise himself by about 6 feet into the

155

air, this was promptly corrected by another of the Llamas who said no ten feet! They were quite serious about it all. At Pamionchi we were at our closest to Kanchenjunga and the snows but were only afforded a very brief glimpse of them – very disappointing as I believe the view is wonderful. From there we went to a lovely little place set in a valley about 5000 feet up, it rather reminded me of the Langdale Valley. Then came our big day, 18 miles and a climb to over 12000 feet, ending up at about that height at a place called Phalut which you can find on any map because the bungalow is exactly where Bengal, Sikkim & Nepal all meet. We arrived in thick mist & some of our coolies, 2 girls as a matter of fact, did not get in until long after dark which was a bit disturbing. The next morning dawned perfectly clear & we were all up to see the sun rise. That is almost impossible to describe. From 12000 feet we commanded all the close hills divided by valleys in Nepal, Sikkim & Bengal. Behind them is a mountain wall, covering an exact semicircle round you as you look North. The 180° of wall is nearly all snow covered throughout its extent, and towering up on the wall are two separate and massive snowy ranges, one Kanchenjunga to the North and the other Everest and its neighbouring peaks to the N.W. Everest itself looks not so high as some of the neighbouring peaks since it stands a little back, but even from 70 miles away it was most impressive. The sun catches the top of Kanchenjunga, only about 20 miles, then as it spreads out over Kanchenjunga it gets the top of the other mountains round Everest & then, almost like putting on a light, the whole side of Everest glows while the other mountains round are still dark except for their tips. Everest catches the light first not because of its few extra hundred feet so much as the way it is facing but it is most impressive all the same. Opposite Everest on the semicircle, to the East of the Kanchenjunga range is a single snowy peak which looked almost transparent in the sun, Chummel Hari, the sacred mountain of Tibet. We rested a whole day at Phalut, perfect views all the morning though as nearly always happened it clouded a bit in the afternoon; then for the next 2 days we kept to the peaks, the end of the first day providing perhaps an even more wonderful view than from Phalut. I will write a continuation of this letter tomorrow.

I duly wrote again on 22 October 1944:

. . . Bye the bye, for Llama in my previous letter read Lama throughout – I have just been reading *Lost Horizon* again is which reminded me I had spelt it wrongly. I think I left you in my last letter at Phalut where Sikkim, Nepal & Bengal adjoin. 12000 feet up and very cold at night, however plenty of wood for fires and some fine bellows to blow them up with. We had 2 nights there (spending one free day lazing about) and then walked South along a ridge keeping high all the way. It was that day, about our seventh out, that we saw our first white faces, 17 Rover Scouts drawn from the R.A.F. and Army in Bengal and doing the same route the other way round. The war news was only about 4 days old – quite exciting, and we stopped and talked with just about all of them on the way. That night we spent at Sandakpoo, only a very little lower than Phalut and if anything an even finer view. We again saw the sun rise but I will not describe that again, not that I have succeeded as it is. The next and last full day we had two quite entertaining incidents. I was walking with Jim when I suddenly saw the blue poppy growing [my mother had some of this rare plant growing in Lloran House garden which had originally come from the Himalayas and of which she was very proud]. We had to scramble down a minor precipice to get to it but succeeded in doing so. There were only two plants, both rather taller than they grow at home, and past their best though there were still several flowers. Anyway we collected some seeds which I will send you in due course, then if they come up you can say 'oh yes, my son sent them from the Himalayas.' Anyway perhaps a little fresh infusion into your stock might be good. I have since asked Mr Fawcus, who is a great authority on all things Himalayan and is staying here and is also a natural historian, he said it is rare to see it growing outside Tibet. He was very surprised I had seen it growing where I had – certainly they were the only ones we found. In the main flowers were rather disappointing – this of course is not a good time of year for them, though there were plenty of wild flowers of a kind it would not be worth while sending you. The second amusing incident was the girl on the horse whom we met that day escorted by two officers. Ken and Peter Hudson, the Bombardier in the party, were about a mile in front and she knew Peter quite well. She met Jim and me about half an hour after that and as soon as she saw me she said 'I know you, your name is Maurice' – a conversational opening I always find very disconcerting. Apparently she had been a nurse at Mary's – name of Mary Bigmore – Tim may remember her, I am afraid I did not. About a mile behind us was our fifth member of the party, Frank Ayrey, a Lieutenant Colonel and medical specialist and this girl is now working at the same hospital as he is and so she knew him too. I think the escorting officers began to get a bit upset by the way she knew every man she met in such a remote part of the world.

You will probably have heard how we took with us the Colonel and the bombardier I have just mentioned; we were a bit intrigued about such an odd mixture, Lt-Cols & bombardiers do not usually have much chance for making close friends, however the common ground was play acting, the two had more or less produced a play together. They were an entertaining pair and Frank Ayrey I am glad to say is staying on here until I go which I shall do on Saturday next. Peter Hudson, the bombardier, is a budding poet and composer, he has already written two concertos, and is by profession a publisher, his father being a master printer which interested me. The coolies we took I have not mentioned yet, a very good crowd, 10 and a head man who also cooked, two of the ten being girls! That is the normal practice, though it seems a bit barbarous to have a little girl of 14 to carry your luggage over high mountains. I am having a very pleasant time now just idling in Darjeeling and living in comfort.

I wrote again on Saturday, 28 October; everything was packed and I was about to catch the mountain train from Darjeeling en route for Calcutta. I had found plenty of old friends staying in Darjeeling.

The weather has been perfect, really glorious days with magnificent views. I have not been unduly energetic though one day I walked with someone right up above Darjeeling to where one could get a very good view of the snows with Mackaloo, one of the peaks close to Everest, just appearing. Usually the afternoons are misty up here but this week it has often been clear all day and there have been some grand sunsets when the snows of Kanchenjunga turn to rose. This club is really a very pleasant place to stay at, while I hear the Windamere where I was before has lapsed terribly now, not a patch on what it used to be. Last night I went to a cocktail party at Mrs Synge's where Jim and Ken and I stayed before starting off.

In the course of this letter I also said I would be spending a day or two in Calcutta as I was not due back on my train until the following Thursday.

By 5 November I was back on the train, delighted with my large post and especially all the magazines I had been sent for my patients to read.

My journey back was an easy one. I stayed in Calcutta at the same place as on my trip up, arriving on Sunday morning and leaving on Wednesday evening. . . Calcutta was about as plentifully supplied with old friends as on my outward trip, including two Mary's people I had not seen before. . . I returned here on Thursday evening choosing a station on my piece of line where I knew not many people would be travelling to and so getting a more comfortable journey. The journey included 8 hours in a very comfortable river steamer which was most pleasant; I think river steamer is the pleasantest form of all travel but of course loses the advantage of speed which air gives you. I fetched up here on Thursday afternoon and by great good luck there was my train in the station, I had no idea where it would be on the route and thought it might be 24 hours or more before I caught up with it.

Everything was slack, I have returned to an existence of long lazy days bathing and lying in the sun though I am having a trip today. However as the train is about to have some repairs done life is going to be even lazier unless I find some job to occupy myself with while they are being done. I feel anyway my time is drawing to a close with this unit.

By 12 November after dealing with various bits of news I had received from home I continued:

I don't know quite what I shall do for the next few weeks. My train is being overhauled starting the day after tomorrow and that means we shall have to move off it. I have arranged to farm most of my staff out at a military hospital and shall probably go to one myself and ask for a ward to occupy my time. The trouble is the hospitals are very slack just now. I am tired of long days doing nothing and hope to get a new job fairly soon now. It does seem absurd that for the last 3 months I have done virtually no work at all while Tim is frantically busy. I shall have to send someone 200 miles (400 there and back) to pick up my mail from now on so there may be some delay, however I will send him every fourth day or so. [I was now in Dacca – my mail went to the ambulance train HQ at Chittagong.] Most of my British staff I am firmly sending to the Himalayas for leave, my sergeant major is now in Calcutta fixing up accommodation for them.

By 19 November I found myself staying in the 17th BGH in Dacca. The hospital was very slack at this time and I had to content myself with wandering round the wards looking at any interesting cases that were in. As I explained in my letter I was completely my own master but it was difficult to find enough to do to occupy my time – 'You really should write to me as Major Maurice R.A.M.C. (Retd) I feel.' However Dacca did have a good club with a swimming pool and library; and there was the cinema where I saw *Random Harvest*. Although I had no work in the hospital the mess was a pleasant one and contained three Old Marlburians. The weather in Dacca at the end of November was very pleasant and I attended the races on 25 November. I am no betting man and was a bit cross when the hospital padre insisted on buying tickets at the tote for one race and we were to share the proceeds – or losses. However my anger was dissipated when we each gained £2 on a total stake of fifteen shillings.

On 2 December I wrote home acknowledging and commenting on a large and somewhat premature Christmas post and then continued:

My posting is likely to arrive literally at any minute. Although I always used to say I would never become a D.A.D.M.S. it did seem fairly inevitable from here and when I was asked 3 months ago if I would return to 4 Corps in that capacity after some initial hesitation I agreed. On getting used to the idea I became quite keen because as those jobs go it is considered a plum of the first order and carries the interest of a war if not of medicine – so much better than being in a back area. On my way through Calcutta on leave I met the man at present doing that job and he greeted the idea with some enthusiasm – he wanted a command somewhere as a Lieut-Colonel. Since then everybody seems to have agreed that I should do that job – and this morning I heard from H.Q. I had been the subject of a D.O. (demi-official letter) from General Thompson, the D.M.S. asking for my appointment. Now the present man is going on a month's leave which means being away for over 2 months and so the telephone wires have begun to hum and soon my orders will be through. Officially the appointment is temporary, but I do not imagine Johnson, whose place I take, will return to it. Anyway I am off the train and I am sure I will not return there. Tomorrow if I can I will go to Calcutta and store some surplus kit, which means getting back on Tuesday, but if I get an urgent signal to move that may not be possible.

The only thing that worries me is that there has been so much fuss about my going back to 4 Corps and so many people have been concerned in getting me there that I am afraid much more will be expected of me than I can give. I know nothing of administration and am sadly lacking in knowledge of army routine and am going to one of the 4 most important jobs a major (R.A.M.C.) can do in the 14 Army. On the other hand I do know the clerks in the office and they are very good and I hope will steer me through the many pitfalls I see ahead. It is sad my old friend the D.D.M.S. 4 Corps left some time ago but I believe his successor is a very good fellow though I have never met him. Anyway there will still be a number of old friends there which gives me a big start.

I concluded this letter by wishing everyone a happy Christmas and wondering what chance I had of celebrating Christmas 1945 in Marlborough.

CHAPTER IX

Return to 4 Corps – Defeat of the Japanese – Home

I have based these memoirs of my war years very largely on extracts taken from my letters home. The letters written from Burma as a staff officer can say very little about my activities and much of what I wrote is not of great interest. Sadly the last letter I have is dated 3 March; what can have happened to the succeeding ones I do not know, but I do have some interesting and amusing memories, anecdotes which I could not have written in my letters home anyway. I also have quite a detailed 'Medical History of 4 Corps – 1945' which in fact was largely written by me and typed by my clerks in my office tent near Pegu some twenty-five miles north of Rangoon at the end of the campaign. As I was asked to write it I presume it was filed somewhere in the old War Office.

I suppose my two greatest interests in life have been doctoring and travel; now the latter was to take precedence, but I did find my work as a staff officer, organizing supplies for the medical units, air evacuation of casualties and the constant moves to which we were all being continuously subjected intensely interesting; I count myself very lucky to have had the experience.

On 11 December my address was once more 4 Corps HQ, SEAC. I had gone to Calcutta by land and as usual met many old friends there. 'The man whom I have taken this job over from was there among others and was able to hand over to me on the balcony of Calcutta's leading restaurant!' I managed to store a lot of my belongings at Thomas Cook's and next day flew to Comilla where I lunched with a friend and then flew on to Imphal. I spent the night there in a mess with lots of old friends and next day travelled by motor transport to Tamu. This entailed a few miles of flat plain and then the long winding road through mountainous country to the new location of 4 Corps HQ situated in the Kabaw Valley close to Tamu and actually inside the Burma border. I still remember that drive well and the thrill it gave me. We were from now on accommodated in tents and my total gear was limited to 65 lb including the camp bed which I had brought from England and originally purchased for two pounds ten shillings, my fee for completing a cremation certificate while an HP at St Mary's.

In my letter I did write:

The general very amused at my getting back though he knew I was coming. [I had already heard he was destined to leave the Corps himself very shortly.] There are of course many new faces about the place but a fair proportion of old ones too. No one seemed in the least surprised at my getting back, in fact everyone knew I was likely to come about a month ago and some even longer. Of course I knew myself two or three months ago that this was likely to be my destination.

An old friend of Uncle Godfrey's has been in this afternoon, Brigadier Macalevey. He is the one just above my immediate boss. He said he had tried to get in touch with Uncle Godfrey when he was in England a few weeks ago but could not make contact – he knew about his working at Oxford. Very interested in where Jean and Griselda were, but that I find is quite a common interest with senior officers anywhere! Funnily enough he had heard of me from General Scoones but had not realised I was one of the family.

I dined last night with Signals whom I used to mess with in the old days. Very nice to see them all again – really the whole affair has been a sort of minor homecoming – it is nice not to have to start from scratch in a new job but to know people before hand.

My letter continued with comments on news from the home front where the Germans were making their last major stand on the Ardennes front which was causing some degree of anxiety.

My letters did make it quite apparent that I was thoroughly enjoying my new experience. Brigadier Panton had taken over as DDMS from my old boss Brigadier Dymond. David Panton had been a regular officer but a gynaecologist and obstetrician as a specialist at home, for soldiers did have wives. I do not think he was of quite the same calibre as Brigadier Dymond but we got on fine and met regularly after the War. Although he lived in Colchester he visited us in Marlborough and then his son, whom we had also come to know, married and came to live in Seend and so we kept up with him until he died many years later.

Our camp in the Kabaw Valley was very much in the jungle but it was winter – 'quite cool at night and pleasant during the day. There is a lovely clear stream to bathe in with a number of pools deep enough for swimming. I do not manage to get a bathe every day even though it is only 5 minutes to the stream, but usually get one on alternate days.' The reason for my excessive workload at this time was on account of new orders from 14th Army. It had been thought that the Japanese would try to hold out on the Schwebo plain north of Mandalay and west of the Irrawaddy but captured Japanese documents showed their defence was going to be concentrated round Mandalay and to the south of the Irrawaddy (Map – p. 174). This would enable them to push us back wherever we attempted a crossing – 4 Corps had been destined to cross the Chindwin with 33 Corps and fight on the Schwebo plain; now General Slim wisely decided to make a major change of plan. Instead of crossing the Chindwin 4 Corps would advance south down the dust road along the Gangaw valley on the west side of Burma and force a crossing to the south and many miles from Mandalay, and capture Meiktila, the main administrative centre of the Japanese 15th and 33rd Armies. This was to involve a 300-mile journey for 4 Corps over a most difficult road through mountainous country and then force the river crossing. As I wrote in my Medical History of 4 Corps 'The whole of this advance was to be carried out with as little ostentation as possible, deluding the enemy into believing that at most only a division was against them on that road and

168

that 4 Corps was still in North Burma. This was the deception plan; its success was proved on the battle fields of Meiktila.'

On 15 December, my birthday as it happens, an event took place at Imphal which I would dearly have loved to witness. The King had given special permission for the Viceroy – Lord Wavell had succeeded Lord Linlithgow – to knight General Slim and his three Corps Commanders on the field of battle. Mountbatten's diaries were published in 1988 and on 15 December he wrote:

> heard for the first time in my life the remarkable order – Lieutenant Generals – quick march! – Bill Slim and Geoffry Scoones were in the Gurkha Rifles; Monty Stopford was in the Rifle Brigade, and poor Christison was the only heavy infantryman present and so he had the greatest difficulty keeping up with the fast rifle step. The opportunity was missed of saying – Lieutenant Generals – form fours – which might have made the occasion even more unique.

All this led to 14th Army getting a little more publicity from the BBC which was good and in a letter dated 23 December I was able to write 'General Scoones departure to be G.O.C. in C. Central Command has also been announced. He did not seem to like the idea of going though one would have thought after 2 years he might have been pleased and anyway it means promotion.' He had a very distinguished post-war career and finished as High Commissioner in New Zealand. The new Commander of 4 Corps was

Lieutenant General Messervy; Slim held him in high regard and under him 4 Corps did achieve the difficult target it had been set. I had no dealings with him; I do believe those comparatively few officers who had served for long and closely to Scoones took less warmly to Messervy. Scoones liked people who stood up and argued with him, Messervy did not tolerate opposing views; this was a point made to me quite recently by an officer who had served close to both. Certainly it was Scoones who regularly attended the 4 Corps reunions until he died; Messervy never came to one, but it must be said he was Corps Commander for a much shorter period.

On Christmas Day 4 Corps HQ made its first move, a move of nearly 100 miles along the dust road into and some way up the Gangaw valley to another jungle site with the Myitha river flowing nearby. This was the first of many moves but my letters home could tell nothing about them except that I did comment on 31 December: 'Travelling on Burma roads has cured me of any desire for movement on them. The dust is appalling and one arrives black and blue at ones destination.' However we were getting plentiful supplies of very good food; I did comment on that! In fact after the first two moves virtually all my travel was by air, a much more comfortable way of getting around in those conditions. The Corps had now become so organized that it always had a landing strip made large enough to take Dakotas or Commandos. Casualties from forward areas could only be evacuated by light plane – L5s – which could carry only one casualty at a time; there were no helicopters in those days. Medical units (and Corps HQ) were grouped close to these airstrips hacked out of the jungle and only the more serious cases were evacuated by heavy planes to the base hospitals in India. Now that we had suppressive mepacrine malaria was much less of a problem and anyway it was the non-malarial season. Battle casualties were comparatively light; not much attempt was being made by the Japanese to hold up what was thought to be a light diversionary force – they were concerned with what they assumed would be the main attack aimed at Mandalay. I was concerned with the organization of all these affairs which I did find most fascinating.

On 7 January 1945 I did comment on the weather.

One always expects rain for a few days at this time of year and we are having it now. Six feet of dust becomes six feet of mud and you can imagine the result. However I am reasonably comfortable considering my little all weighs only 65 lbs and I can lie in bed listening to the rain and thinking of far worse nights spent for pleasure at Cranmere Pool.

On several occasions I had hiked to Cranmere Pool on Dartmoor with the College scouts. Later in this letter I commented on the news from Europe:

It appears that the Western Front is going a bit better now but I suppose we cannot hope for a quick victory yet. It is extraordinary how self centred one becomes about the war news – Europe seems as far from here now and as comparatively unimportant as this show must to people at home.

On 15 January I wrote saying I had received quite a good impression of Sir Alexander Hood – the Director General of the Army Medical Services – who had visited our HQ and was interesting on the subject of repatriation and release of doctors, 'but by the look of things I am due for a long time in the army yet.' In the same letter I wrote 'I suppose the College will celebrate the new Archbishop suitably.' The announcement of his appointment had just been made – Archbishop Fisher was an OM and his sons had all been at Marlborough. 'Harry Fisher was over here the other day but I missed seeing him. He is on 14 Army staff as a Lieutenant Colonel and I gather they expect him to back up the war here with a series of miracles.' I teased him about this when I bumped into him in the High Street some time ago.

In my next letter dated 21 January I did ask for some books to be sent to me – reading throughout the war was my great relaxation and weight had prevented me from bringing anything more than Wilkie Collins *The Woman in White* with me and I had nearly finished it. On 29 January I was able to write a rather more interesting letter. After acknowledging various letters received and commenting on the number of OMs on the Corps staff I said how grateful I was to Sir Rayner Goddard, soon to be Lord Chief Justice. My cousin Jim was married to his daughter and he had heard I had lost my pipe in the jungle and was sending me a replacement; pipes were not easy to come by anywhere in those days. I continued:

> The main reason for not writing yesterday was because I have been away for 24 hours. I flew back to India yesterday morning and returned by plane again this morning. I feel myself to be deep in Burma here and it is amazing to get back so quickly. A lovely trip, the mountains are very high on the India Burma frontier and one skims across some of the peaks with still higher ones on either side – fascinating country to fly over. I went to one of the places [this was in fact Comilla where 14th Army HQ was still based] I used to pass through in my train and looked for it as we circled over head but it was not there. I had not much time to do all I wanted and so would not have been able to do much about it even if it had been in, but I should have liked to have collected a few more of my belongings off it. I stayed last night at a hospital in this place. Philip Willcox, whom I last saw in Calcutta a few months ago also turned up in the evening having come in by air and on his way somewhere else. Off at crack of dawn and back in my office before 10 a.m., amazing this flying business is really. Otherwise I have not done much of note this week. I usually manage to get about a couple of hours round about tea time for a bathe which keeps me fit and is well worth while. The weather is lovely, very different from what you are getting in England by all accounts though cool at night. . . The Russian news is getting better every day, it really looks as if the Germans will have to call it a day soon. Incidentally entertainments here are terrific now. I think I saw two cinema shows last week, mobile

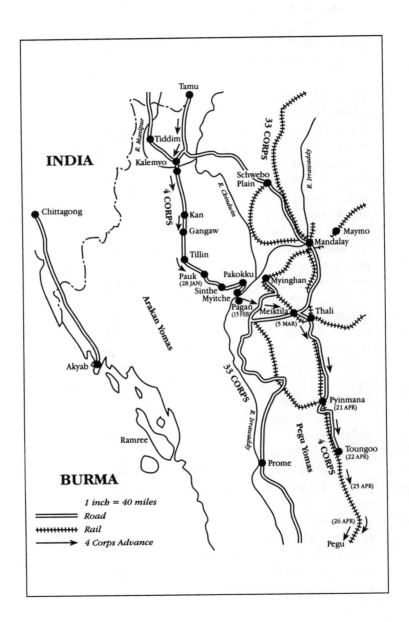

INDIA

Chittagong

BURMA

1 inch = 40 miles
━━━━ Road
+++++++ Rail
──▶ 4 Corps Advance

Tamu

Tiddim

R. Manipur

Kalemyo

4 CORPS

Kan

Gangaw

Tillin

Pauk
(28 JAN)

Sinthe

Myitche

Pakokku

Pagan
(15 FEB)

R. Chindwin

Schwebo
Plain

33 CORPS

R. Irrawaddy

Maymo

Mandalay

Myinghan

Meiktila
(5 MAR)

Thali

Arakan Yomas

Akyab

Ramree

33 CORPS

R. Irrawaddy

Prome

Pyinmana
(21 APR)

Pegu Yomas

4 CORPS

Toungoo
(22 APR)

(25 APR)

(26 APR)

Pegu

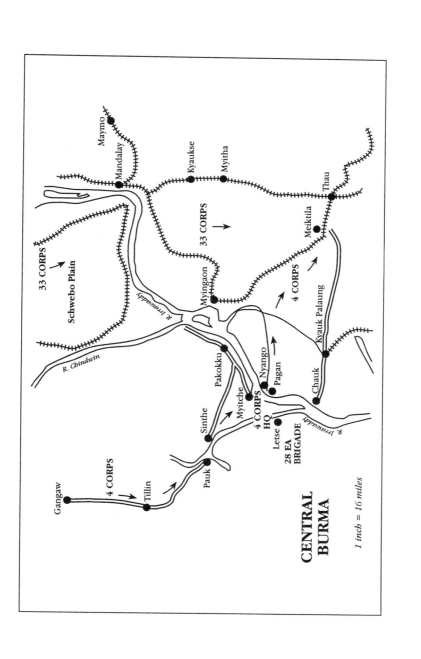

CENTRAL
BURMA

1 inch = 16 miles

cinema, first class screen and very good tone, and also an ENSA show. Another ENSA show in a day or two. This front is different from what it used to be.

In a letter dated 4 February I remarked for once things were quite slack – 'almost a Sunday hush over the place at the moment'. I had apparently had another letter from Rayner Goddard all about the steps he was taking to get me a pipe; they were not easily come by in the War. In the course of quite a long letter I wrote that another Old Marlburian was temporarily living in our mess and then continued:

> I poked my head into an office here the other day while looking for someone and found Michael O'Regan sitting inside. We did not have much time to talk then but he looked in for tea in my mess yesterday (which made 4 Marlburians in that one mess alone). He seems just the same and was very amused to hear I had been meeting Tony Hallows. I should think Michael will be in and out quite often now. He assured me he had written to Mrs O'Regan only 3 days ago, though he added he had said in that letter he was going to be too busy to write again for a month – which I said was sheer nonsense! I shall hope to reply to Tim's letter before very long. Tell him that Ronnie Shaw, one time anaesthetist at Mary's, turned up the other day. I had sent him out into the jungle on mules which he seemed to have thoroughly enjoyed.

In the course of my letter written on 11 February I said pressure of work was increasing steadily.

This has been a very hectic week indeed with a lot of travelling to and fro. Three days running I had to travel by air, it would save a lot of trouble really if I could have a private aeroplane! Still it is all very interesting really and I enjoy getting about like I do. In the old days, in fact always until I came here this job was purely an office one, but now I am roping in someone else to do the paper work.

I now had a staff captain to deal with the office work. He was Alexis Brook and he told me he had a Russian mother. He also said he had a younger brother, Peter, who was making his name as a theatrical producer at home which seemed a bit strange to me. Peter Brook has indeed made a great name for himself, among other achievements *Whose Who* states that he is now a director and co-producer of the Royal Shakespeare Theatre. Alexis was a great person to have beside me; he became a consultant psychiatrist in London and was amused to see me in his audience when I was doing a refresher course in London many years later. In this same letter I wrote:

> I ran into Michael O'Regan again this week, yesterday in fact, I had just landed on an air field and he was there with a lot of trucks, just what I wanted, but he would not part with one! ... This letter has taken me 3 hours to write to date – this particular sentence 10 minutes with 3 telephone calls and one person to see me! I think I will finish it off in the morning.
>
> Feb 12. I am feeling a good deal brighter this morning, it is really the best time for writing between

177

8-30 and 9 before the telephone gets really busy. I am sorry about the Williamsons having their house so badly damaged. Bathing is off for me for the time being which is rather a blow, I hope it will be practicable again before long but I think it is likely to become more difficult. I am afraid even this part of the letter is pretty disconnected but it has taken me 35 minutes to write this far this morning and I will bring this to a close.

It is apparent from my letters home that I was thoroughly enjoying myself and was not suffering any particular hardship, nothing much wrong in living in a tent in North Burma's winter climate. Our advance up the Gangaw Valley was led by the Lushai Brigade, a brigade which – to quote Slim – had originally been hurriedly improvised from certain spare Indian battalions and some local levies to prevent Japanese infiltration into the Lushai Hills. The Lushai Brigade had been in contact with the Japanese for a long time in the hills around Tiddim and it was hoped if they led our advance the Japanese would not realise that 4 Corps was behind them rather than far to the east with 33 Corps. This hope happily was fulfilled.

By chance quite recently while on holiday in Ibiza I mentioned to a retired solicitor who has made his home there and is an old acquaintance that I was writing my war memoirs. In the course of conversation I learned that he had been the Brigade Major in the Lushai Brigade and was leading a much less comfortable life advancing down the dusty – and sometimes muddy – track fighting the Japanese. They were dependent entirely on air drop for supplies. Only ammunition and medical supplies were dropped by parachute, everything else came down in free fall and there was the never-ending risk of being underneath as the heavy cases descended from the skies.

By the beginning of February 4 Corps advance troops were approaching the Irrawaddy – opposition being comparatively light owing to the success of Slim's deception plan; 4 Corps HQ remained of course in the rear and all my advances were made by air. It had been a busy time getting our forward medical units in position but this was fully accomplished by 15 February; the 7th Division actually began their crossing on 14 February. Faulty engines on the boats caused more trouble than the Japanese for the first few days and I was writing home on 18 February that I had had a much quieter week; I had even had time to send more money back to Mr Palmer – Lloyds Bank Manager – to invest. 'I feel by the time I get home again I will be toying with the idea of buying Littlecote!' I told how the weather was very pleasant and Brigadier Panton and I had packed up early and gone for a long walk to a lovely stream for a bathe; I remember that afternoon well after all these years. 'This is a very open air sort of life and since I seldom wear a shirt I am beginning to get very brown.'

A letter written on 25 February is of no particular interest and the last letter that I have is dated 3 March; thereafter I have to rely on my memory and the account I wrote of the Medical History of 4 Corps. The letter of 3 March is quite long, and I will give some quotes from it but naturally I could not say that two days before writing it 4 Corps had moved to Myitche, on the banks of the Irrawaddy and opposite Pagan with its incredible pagodas, although on the latter I do comment.

> The weather is becoming increasingly hot here. I reckon this year I am going to experience real heat, very different from the comparatively mild heat of Bengal and Assam, though I did not regard it as mild at the time. Anyway with any luck this will be my last hot weather, three are quite enough. One trouble is we cannot wear shorts. There are so many infernal diseases around that shorts are completely forbidden though one can work without a shirt during the day. . . Lady Louis Mountbatten was round here recently though I did not see her myself. She certainly does get around, Brigadier Panton said she told him she got over the German lines once by mistake in the Arnhem direction and the plane was hit putting one engine out of action and wounding a nurse who was sitting beside her. Burma is the most astonishing place with its pagodas, they really are the most extraordinary structures, I wish I could get more time to look at them myself, I am afraid we are smashing the place up to a large extent; I would hate to be liberated myself and one wonders what the local inhabitants must think about it all. Still they do not seem unfriendly on the whole and are extremely anxious to sell you food in the form of chicken, eggs and fruit though like the Manipuris and unlike the general population of India they never beg.

I believe it was in our camp close to Myitche that I had one rather unpleasant experience. We had been warned about the prevalence of snakes in Burma and were always made to wear boots when walking. One evening I entered my tent and found a viper sitting on a box under my table. How I dealt with the situation I do not remember.

There now ensued a rapid advance to Meiktila which was over sixty miles south-east of the crossing at Myitche. A wide bridgehead had been established and the advance was led by a new division – 17th Indian Division – which had been flown in to increase the numbers of 4 Corps divisions to three. By 1 March this division was within two miles of the town. By 5 March Meiktila had been taken but Kimura – the Japanese general commanding all their forces in Burma – realized how he had been misled into believing Mandalay was our main objective and so withdrew many of his forces from that area to fight 4 Corps round Meiktila. Throughout March the battle raged, casualties were heavy and life for me exceptionally busy but I did have the great satisfaction of meeting the urgent requirements of the various forward medical units in the field. I suppose I was getting a bit above myself in the general excitement; I remember once telling Brigadier Panton that I thought he ought to go and visit a certain forward Field Ambulance to make sure their requirements were being met; he looked at me rather ruefully and said, 'Are you trying to get me killed?' I am sure he went just the same. Fighting round the airstrip at Meiktila was particularly fierce and an improvised surgical team had to fly there on 19 March. On 23 March the enemy had an anti-tank gun firing down the airstrip from one end; after a heavy plane loaded with casualties was put out of action – fortunately without loss of life – we had to return to evacuation by light aircraft to the main medical centre close to our HQ at Myitche. My concern was with the flying out of casualties and getting supplies to the medical units.

My records show 226 casualties were brought in by light plane to the medical centre at Myitche on 26 March – 171 on the long hop from Meiktila of which 157 were actual battle casualties. We established two theatres and three surgical teams at Meiktila and four theatres with four teams at Myitche. By 30 March we had again got full control of the airstrip at Meiktila and evacuation could again proceed normally by heavy aircraft.

'With the battle for Meiktila won the campaign entered a new phase. 33 Corps had captured Mandalay and as the hammer to 17 Div's anvil had squeezed out the enemy North of Meiktila, causing what was left of their battered remnants to retreat into the hills.' A quote from my Medical History of 4 Corps written at Pegu in May 1945. 'Then as disruption spread out from Meiktila 33 Corps must be loosed in an all out offensive to the South – the hammer to the anvil.' A quote from Field Marshal Slim's *Defeat into Victory* published in 1956!

Our next objective was to advance to Rangoon but as Slim was to write in his book it was going to be a race against two tough competitors, the enemy and the monsoon. The monsoon normally breaks about 15 May and the distance from Meiktila was great. The railway route from Meiktila to Rangoon is 320 miles – via the Irrawaddy Valley well to the west of the railway it is 370 miles; the Pegu Yomas separated a long stretch of the two routes. If the monsoon broke before our forces had reached Rangoon all our landing grounds, which were only grass strips, would be lost, the roads would dissolve and the health of the troops would be in great jeopardy. 4 Corps were chosen to undertake the railway route while 33 Corps which had previously been to the east of us were given the Irrawaddy Valley to the west. 4 Corps' advance was led by 5th and 17th Divisions with the 19th Division following up behind. 4 Corps HQ moved to Meiktila on 4 April – as always by air. Meiktila had been almost totally destroyed; 4 Corps HQ was established beside one of the two large lakes which lay to the north and south of the town. This was excellent for me as I was able to swim every day without taking any time over it.

While at Meiktila General Slim made one of his frequent visits to our Headquarters but on this occasion he was accompanied by Lady Slim who wished to visit the local medical units. Brigadier Panton asked me to meet Lady Slim at the airfield and conduct her to our Headquarters and he would then take her round. I suspect he did this as he thought it would be a kind act to allow me to meet General Slim. Thus it was I found myself standing beside the landing ground with General Messervy and a group of senior

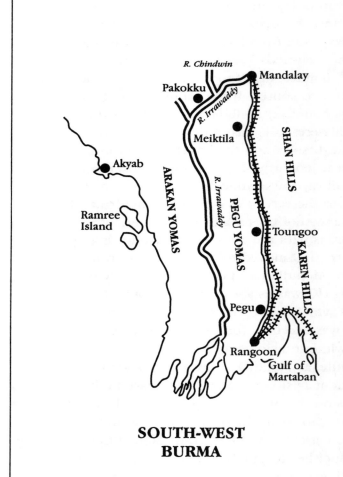

SOUTH-WEST BURMA

officers as the plane landed. I was introduced to Sir William and it was explained that I was to take charge of his wife. He seemed a bit taken aback that such a young officer should have been detailed to meet Lady Slim and as we shook hands he said, 'You will look after her, won't you.' I duly took her over and we went back to our headquarters where I handed her over to David Panton; I rather think he got a bit of a rocket from Messervy for not having been to the airfield himself.

I believe it was at Meiktila that I was becoming increasingly worried by a skin rash which I had developed some time previously and appeared to be affecting my whole body. It was extremely irritating but there was not much that I could do about it and I firmly held the belief of those pre-NHS days that the best speciality to go into was that of dermatology – your patients never called you out at night, never got any better and never died.

With the battle of central Burma won the Japanese were really defeated but they refused to give in and we not only had them but also the threat of the approaching monsoon which could seriously disrupt the advance to Rangoon. Our advance south was held up at Pyabwe – some twenty miles from Meiktila – for the first ten days of April. However this cost the Japanese some 2,000 dead while our casualties were comparatively light. Toungoo – roughly halfway to Rangoon – was captured on 22 April which gave us a good airstrip. By 29 April our forward troops were approaching Pegu, some forty miles north of Rangoon and where the Japanese made their last stand. Meanwhile 4 Corps HQ had moved to Toungoo. A young Indian officer, a major, was temporarily attached to our mess and I was asked to accommodate him in my sleeping tent. By this time my skin was becoming very much worse and I do not think he was at all happy at sharing a tent with such a manifestly diseased officer – it might even be leprosy! My tent companion was in fact the Maharajah of Cooch Bihar – his sister was married to the Maharajah of Jaipur.

There was heavy fighting in and around Pegu during the last few days of April and early May complicated by the monsoon breaking two weeks early, on 1 May, thus putting the airstrips out of action. However Pegu was firmly in our hands by March when a fully operational medical unit was moved in. By 9 May the weather had improved and the surrounding airstrips were again fully operational and casualty evacuation could proceed normally. Meanwhile the Japanese had evacuated Rangoon, a fact that was first noted by one of our pilots flying over the City and seeing the slogan on the roof of the gaol 'JAPS GONE EXTRACT DIGIT'. 4 Corps HQ was established at Pegu in early May; the town itself was a shambles and permeated by the stink of unburied Japanese dead; fortunately we were camped just outside.

With the temporary lull in the monsoon I had acquired the use of a two-seater light plane – an L5; it had an American pilot and I enjoyed flipping round the country visiting units. Although we had got to Rangoon the actual line that we held was only about two miles wide down the railway line from Meiktila and not all that much wider down the Irrawaddy Valley which had been the scene of the advance of 33 Corps. Right across Burma parties of Japanese were streaming like ants to escape to the east. One day Brigadier Panton came into my office tent with a somewhat worried look on his face – he had been instructed to produce a Medical History of 4 Corps in 1945. I at once volunteered to write the main part dealing with the organization of the medical units and the evacuation of the sick and wounded during our advance through Burma. There were two sections at the end dealing with the health of the troops written by the staff officer responsible for hygiene and the malarial statistics written by the staff officer whose whole-time concern was for anti-malarial measures.

Strangely I have no memory of VE Day – 7 May – we were much too busy to have a celebration over a war which for long had not concerned us. However I did manage to take a few days off during May and flew up to Mandalay and spent two or three nights in a hotel in a hill station which was still functioning and was far from any Japanese retreating forces. Meanwhile my skin continued to cause me great discomfort and one day I flew up to 14th Army Headquarters, which was then at Meiktila, to ask the opinion of the consultant dermatologist attached to 14th Army. He was very indecisive as to diagnosis or treatment but did whisper to me that cases had been reported of skin sensitivity to the anti-malarial drug mepacrine which we were all taking. He said it was top secret that any harm could come from mepacrine; the suppression of malaria had contributed much to the success of the Burma campaign. If the troops knew of any ill affects apart from turning us all yellow (already rumours had been circulating that it caused impotence) great harm would ensue. At this time it was expected that there would be another year of fighting in the tropics before the Japanese would be defeated. However he went on to assure me that he was certain my trouble was not caused by mepacrine and being a good medical officer I continued with my daily dose.

The flight to Meiktila had been made in quite good weather but on the way back that afternoon in the two-seater L5 we encountered a monsoon storm. We continued to battle our way through thunder, lightning, high winds and driving rain. I was sitting behind the American pilot who suddenly attracted my attention and pointed to the fuel gauge – close on empty! What with the storm, the lack of fuel and the knowledge that there were many escaping Japanese passing underneath I spent the time scribbling out my will just in case someone found my body. However we just managed to reach the airfield at Toungoo and with a full tank and the storm being over resumed our journey to Pegu. On another occasion I found time to visit Rangoon – not much bomb damage but it looked pretty derelict, particularly in the port area. The golden dome of the Schwe Dagon Pagoda looked magnificent from afar but I did not visit it.

With the Medical History of 4 Corps completed and typed by my clerks I felt the time had come for me to go. Sleep was almost impossible because of the irritation and I had developed appalling facial disfigurement. I told David Panton that I could no longer carry on, wrote my own movement order and one day in June boarded a plane bound for Calcutta. After a refuelling stop at Ramree Island we duly landed at the airstrip situated at Barrackpore where I knew the army hospital specializing in skin diseases was situated. There I hired horse-drawn transport to the hospital where I demanded I should be admitted at once. The admitting doctor looked at me somewhat blankly since I had short-circuited all official channels but when he saw my skin at once removed 10 ml of blood to test me for secondary syphilis; I was not amused but General Scoones might have been.

I was duly admitted to the officers' ward where I asked about possible sensitivity to mepacrine. Nothing seemed to be known of this and I was told I must continue my daily dose. After two weeks of sheer misery the medical officer responsible for my treatment developed some ailment himself, he was admitted to my ward and whispered to me to try stopping the mepacrine. Two weeks later and almost overnight the irritation suddenly ceased and I began to shed my skin; I could scrape it off into balls and throw it across the room. It was at this time that Brigadier Mackenna – consultant dermatologist to the British Army and author of a standard text book on skin diseases – arrived with another dermatologist who was consultant to the Indian Army, also a Brigadier. By this time I was the star case in the hospital and they were brought straight to my bed. I opened my pyjama jacket and they stood back in awe as Mackenna exclaimed 'Not even the Americans have got a case as good as this.' I then suffered the indignity of being stripped stark naked, taken onto the ward verandah in full view of a ward containing British other ranks and photographed repeatedly from every direction. However they did tell me I was now unfit for further service in a tropical climate and I would be invalided home. It was while I was in the hospital in Barrackpore that the General Election was taking place. Our votes had to be collected together with those of the forces wherever they were stationed and sent to London; on 26 July we heard the incredible news that the Labour Party had been returned with a considerable majority and Churchill had resigned. If my memory serves me right it was as I was crossing India by train on my way to a transit hospital in Poona that I heard that a new type of bomb, an atomic bomb, had been dropped on Japan, which puts the date as 6 August. On 10 August the second bomb was dropped and the Japanese surrendered, but anyway my war was over.

I have two memories of the Poona hospital where I spent only a short time. On arrival I was shown into a small ward, about eight beds, each with a red blanket on top, just like we used to have at the Old Malthouse. Then I found that Peter Taylor, my old friend of nursery days and who had come to the Malthouse with me, was in the next ward. Could my whole life thereafter have been but a dream? My other memory is of the colonel who was sitting next to me at dinner in the officers' mess that first evening. Not knowing each other, and as sometimes happens at meals, we started talking about drink. He said he came of a very hard-drinking family. I said I came of a very hard-drinking family thinking of one or two of my nine uncles – particularly of Uncle Jack. We had a bit of an argument about this and then I turned to him and said, 'What's your name?' He said 'Maurice – what's yours?' He was my second cousin – another Jack – whom I had met at Chittagong and failed now to recognize. He did have some excuse for not recognizing me as I was so heavily disfigured at the time.

By 14 August I was at sea; I remember little of the voyage home except the heat of the Red Sea and travelling through the Suez Canal which was an experience. I also found a few other sufferers like me who had succumbed to mepacrine. My last memory of the voyage is of seeing for the first time the Rock of Gibraltar. On 27 August we landed at Liverpool and according to my mother's diary I rang home at 1 p.m. and again at 9 p.m. about my plans for getting home. After spending the night at an hotel I caught a train to Oxford and then on to Reading where I was met by my mother and Tim; in fact the diary states I had arrived at the station before they did. After three years less three weeks and to be precise one day I was back in my home town of Marlborough.

Epilogue

The remainder of my army service, inevitably, is anticlimax. After a spell of leave – and no longer a major as my rank had been only temporary – I did a few months first running a casualty clearing station near Blandford and then working in the army barracks at Dorchester. In March I was demobilized and my rank of major was restored to me. I also had to attend a medical board at Swindon and was awarded the miserable sum of about £100 for my mepacrine rash – perhaps the boarding officer felt he could not award me more for he was my uncle Godfrey. In due course I was awarded a Mention in Despatches for my work as DADMS in 4 Corps for the advance to Rangoon.

I then spent six months repolishing my medicine at St Mary's where we returning warriors were paid for doing very little other than work for our University medical degrees – better than the conjoint diplomas with which we had qualified. It was a great time to catch up with old friends and exchange war reminiscences. In June I took my Cambridge MB and then spent six months doing a surgical job at the Royal Devon and Exeter Hospital which I thoroughly enjoyed and escaped some of the worst of the winter snow of 1946/47.

EPILOGUE

In April 1947 I joined the practice in Marlborough. On 15 November I had the great good fortune to marry Second Officer Anne Hony WRNS whom I had been intermittently courting for the last year, intermittently because for the most part we were stationed far apart. No foreign travel was possible in those days and so we spent the first night of our honeymoon in a hotel in the New Forest prior to boarding a plane at Southampton the next day to Jersey. The papers the following morning were full of descriptions of the wedding of the Prime Minister's daughter – Clement Attlee had of course taken over from Churchill. As we had been married the same day we were naturally interested and while lunching at the Polygon Hotel in Southampton were laughing at one of the Sunday tabloids which had a picture of the bride and groom who had appalling protruding front teeth. There was a banner headline with the picture – THEY MUST BE IN LOVE – HE IS THE UGLIEST MAN I HAVE EVER SEEN – Mrs Attlee. Suddenly Anne exclaimed, 'My God – there they are' – lunching at a nearby table. We sat just behind them on the plane to Jersey and I was standing beside him having a wash in the airport loos on arrival. I had ordered a car to take us to our hotel at St Brelades Bay and so I asked him if he would like us to give them a lift; this was declined. Next day we read in the local press they had gone by bus to their boarding house in Commercial Road.